Seriously Selling Services

How to Build a Profitable Services Business in Any Industry

Praise for *Seriously Selling Services*

"*Seriously Selling Services* may be mislabeled, because Alexander does more than show us how to sell services. He starts at the beginning of the process—building services capabilities around products that are fighting against commoditization, dealing effectively with existing channel partners, and evolving the dominant product sales culture to think beyond break-fix support and embrace a new value proposition: services that give customers better performance, faster deployment, and lower cost of ownership. Alexander has paid his dues in the product-to-services transformation club. He draws on years of real-world experience with leading companies to show product companies how to grow with services. *Seriously Selling Services* provides an unmatched, practical road map for senior executives who are ready to execute a serious services strategy."

R. Gary Bridge
Senior Vice President and Global Lead,
Internet Business Solutions Group, Cisco Systems, Inc.

"Jim Alexander does a terrific job in his new book, *Seriously Selling Services*, presenting compelling reasons why senior executives in product companies need to consider selling services. Increased revenue stream, solid profit margins, and enhanced customer loyalty are only a few benefits that selling services can provide. Most importantly, selling services valued highly by customers—implementation, uptime, and professional services—provide market differentiation that will lead to future sales growth for both products and services, despite economic conditions. Jim takes a no-nonsense approach to both the challenges and the rewards of selling high-value services through an impactful writing style that refreshes points made, clearly presents concepts, and gives readers access to best practices for success. I highly recommend this book."

Dolores Kruchten
GM Business Solutions and Services, Vice President, Eastman Kodak Company

"Alexander's suggested approaches and practices really work. We've developed a services-led approach to driving software sales and seen a double-digit increase in margins by implementing the recommendations outlined in his book."

Liz Murphy
Chief Client Officer, Datatel, Inc.

"*Seriously Selling Services* contains just the right mix of theory, best practices, and real-world advice about managing the transition to services. I highly recommend it."

Scott Dysert
Chief Executive Officer, Chromalox

"Jim's rubber-meets-the-road experience shines through as he explains the what, why, and how of becoming successful in services. *Seriously Selling Services* is a must-read for your management staff and everyone in your services organization."

Michael Olmsted
Vice President, Services and Quality, Satisloh, North America

"This is another great book Jim Alexander has written. Built on sound research and real-life experience, Jim's new, challenging, and provocative ideas show you not only how to run a services business profitably and outperform your competitors, but also how to have fun doing it. This is a unique book that considers implementing the change to become service-oriented as fun; it sure is."

Prof. Hans Kasper
School of Business and Economics, Maastricht University, The Netherlands

"If you want to sharpen your business focus, fine-tune your services offerings, and streamline your processes, be sure to add this book to your queue. It is a well-written, practical guide to selling services and a seriously great read!"

Terry Jansen
Founder, PSVillage, and Publisher, Tips from the Trenches: The Collective Wisdom of Over 100 Professional Services Leaders

"Selling services in a product-centric company is no easy task and takes a lot of time, influence, dedication, and perseverance. This topic has been around for a number of years now, and Jim Alexander tackles the issues head-on, highlighting the core dimensions to transitioning to a services-led company. This book reinforces best practices that need to be adopted in order to be successful and provides a holistic approach to seriously selling services. It also provides excellent, usable, practical tools and tips that can be applied quickly. This is a must-read for every services executive who has just started out or is struggling to make inroads in developing a services-led approach in a product-centric company."

Gary Neveling
Alcatel-Lucent, Director, Business Operations
EMEA SBG - Network and System Integration

"Jim did a great job of condensing his many years of experience in service marketing, and shares proven methods to sell services. Unlike many business books, this one is easy to read and reflects Jim's personality and humor. This is a must-read for all your product sales staff who have to transition into the different world of selling services."

John Hamilton
President, Service Strategies Corporation

"This new book compiles over 20 years of professional services wisdom into a must-read for any professional services executive. Not only great content, but told in such a way that is easy to follow and fun to read."

Hank Stroll
Publisher, InternetVIZ B2B Social Media Content and Newsletters

"Jim provided my company with an indispensable set of selling tools developed over decades of successful experience in the professional services industry. He has brought his body of knowledge to the next level with this set of must-read best practices."

Mike Haney
CEO, Athens Group

"This book is definitely worth the read. I specifically found the insightful chapter "Transitioning from Free to Fee" most valuable, because if Alexander's advice is followed, it can transform an unprofitable business into a profitable one."

Claudia Betzner
Executive Director, Service Industry Association

"This book is just like its author—bold and direct in its statements of what can and what can't work in building strong services capabilities. Clear and easy to read, *Seriously Selling Services* is just the right mix of practical theory and real-life experience."

Marc Brûlé
Vice President, Client Services, Halogen Software

"*Seriously Selling Services* is a must-read for executives who are interested in growing sales and profits. Having made the service transition within an electronic controls company, I recognize that the wisdom presented by Mr. Alexander could have saved us a lot of time climbing the learning curve."

Herb Rippe
Former Vice President of Sales, Copeland Corporation

"If you are investing in growing your services business, get serious and invest in this book! Jim's pragmatic advice, industry research, and examples about selling services from his decades of experience on the topic are what you need to get to success faster. His book is laid out in a practical, usable, readable format that makes it easy to digest. You won't regret it."

David C. Munn
President and CEO, ITSMA

Seriously Selling Services

How to Build a Profitable Services Business in Any Industry

James A. Alexander

Thomson-Shore, Inc.

Seriously Selling Services:
How to Build a Profitable Services Business in Any Industry

©2010 James A. Alexander

This edition published by Thomson-Shore, Inc., Dexter, MI.

First Edition

ISBN 978-0-615-32324-4

To my good friend and colleague, Bob Yopko,
a true services champion.

Acknowledgements

Two people have been indispensible in the building of this book.

My thanks to David Rippe, senior consultant at Alexander Consulting and president of Celestia International, for his ongoing insights and suggestions. His feedback definitely improved both the quality and the readability of this book. If you need strategic marketing support, Celestia International is the place to go, and David is the person to talk to.

A boatload of gratitude to my longtime friend and colleague, Suzanne Marie, owner of PagePerfect Creative, for all her many hours of editing, designing, layout, and project management for all aspects of the production of this project. Responsible, reliable, and a hoot to work with—you are the best.

Table of Contents

Foreword

"There is no such thing as common sense. There is only good sense, and it is not common."

As a 30-plus-year services industry executive at four different high-tech companies, I must admit that Jim Alexander's latest book, *Seriously Selling Services: How to Build a Profitable Services Business in Any Industry*, meets the good-sense test. Many authors have written books on how to sell, others have written books on services, and with the ever-increasing global macro-economic role that services are playing, there also are numerous books written on how to sell services, but Jim Alexander's book is different. While it is research-based and includes sound thought leadership, its real value is that it relies heavily on field-proven, real-life scenarios on what works, and equally important, what doesn't work, as a company transitions from a product-led to a services-led company.

In a nutshell, it provides a simple, structured formula for product companies to consider as they embark on a serious transition to services. Additionally, it offers excellent food for thought for companies that are well down the services road, but are yet unable to optimize the results that were promised as they embarked on their own services journey. If these companies are intellectually honest with themselves, they easily can see where they have missed vital steps or made less-than-optimal decisions just by reading Chapters 3 through 5.

Currently we are in a very exciting time in our industry, where both challenges and opportunities abound. There is transformational change happening in the services space that will create the next round of industry-leading companies. The question is: Will your company be one of them—one of those organizations that will realize great return for their shareholders, enjoy great loyalty from their customers, and provide great opportunities for their people?

Jim touches on one of these opportunities when he discusses the Technology Assimilation Gap, which is the gap between the rate at which new technology is introduced into the marketplace and the rate at which the market can assimilate this new technology. The challenge lies in the fact that technology has evolved faster than our customers' ability to utilize it. Notice this isn't about you, it's about the customer; it always has been and always will be. In the end, companies are limiting the size of their opportunities, limiting or losing customer repurchase of their products, and risking market differentiation—none of which are desirable. The reason? They are not focused on ensuring that their customers are getting the full value of what they have been sold. Ask yourself who owns that responsibility in your company. Too often the answer is no one. We sell our customers a solution, provide basic service deliverables, and then wonder why our customer retention rates are lower than expected.

Good delivery is not good enough in the new services world. It will not provide differentiation for your company. At one time services were considered a negative commodity, and the deliverable was just meeting simplistic expectations outlined in basic service level agreements (uptime, response, refresh time). As some companies evolved, they began to view services delivery in a broader sense—the service itself was the product. Today, both of these are just table stakes; necessary, but insufficient in the customer value proposition. The customer's real need is much more holistic: They need to be able to realize the full value of the solution you sold them. In many cases, they do not realize the full value the solution can provide due to its various complexities. This is where the future leaders of services companies will create their strategic differentiation. They will systemically align their people, processes, and technologies to successfully address this gap. This alignment has to include all the personnel within the company who either directly or indirectly touch the customer.

The very tenet that states that everyone sells the organization, its capabilities, and its service offerings is foundational. This is not sales in the traditional sense. Many of these tenets can be found in Alexander's Persuasion Continuum, which focuses on what is good for the client; it is about honest dialogue, not slick presentations; it is about long-term relationships, not short-term transactions; ultimately, it is about becoming the customer's trusted advisor.

The biggest transformation will have to come from an organization's technical talent who traditionally avoid this type of role because it looks and feels too much like pure sales. According to Alexander, there are many reasons why training technical support personnel to sell services should be on your "vital few" list. Why? These professionals can provide the manpower to help the organization scale quickly, they already know the customer and are seen as trusted advisors, their organizational processes and their utilization of technology and knowledge management systems are typically more skilled than others who are in customer-facing roles, and they usually have a cost-effective infrastructure in place due to the extensive cost emphasis over the past decade. In essence, the service culture itself can enable customers to bridge the Technology Assimilation Gap. Although this concept will be foreign to many within your company and will require a retooling of the workforce, this transformation of delivery personnel will be critical to your organization's success.

All of this sounds easy, but it is not, and *Seriously Selling Services* provides a step-by-step process for moving your company toward becoming a true services-led organization. It is a difficult road, but the rewards are great for your shareholders, your customers, and your employees.

Good luck on your journey!

William Steenburgh
Senior Vice President, Xerox Services
Xerox

Introduction

Finding new, profitable streams of revenue—this is one of the prime objectives of almost every executive on the planet. But the choices are few, the challenges big, and the results often mixed. Who has not suffered through a difficult merger or acquisition? How often have the projected benefits of new market strategies never been accomplished?

However, business leaders in many product companies are discovering that selling services cannot only meet this goal of delivering new, profitable growth, but also sell more products at the same time. Is it simple? No. Is it easy? Of course not. Is it worth the effort? You bet.

Thoughtful leaders willing to learn from the mistakes and successes of others and follow the recommendations outlined in this book will be able to successfully sell services, and new, profitable growth will be their reward.

The Marvelous Opportunity

Select companies within a variety of industries are highly successful at selling services. These product companies receive 25% to 55% (44% on average) of their total revenue from services at profit margins the same or better than product profit margins. Furthermore, the product companies that are the best at selling services grow their services revenue 25% faster at margins twice as high as their competitors. Obviously services are an integral component of success for these businesses, not to mention numerous other benefits I'll describe shortly.

Challenges

Yet, with 46% of the executives from the product company I researched (Alexander, 2004) saying that building services was a business priority, why then are many product companies reluctant to aggressively sell services, and some even prefer to give services away? The truth is that although the potential rewards of selling services are great, many things must gel to make it work. In addition, there are multiple potholes on the path to profitable services growth. Finally, these challenges are exacerbated by some misconceptions about services that either stop serious conversations about selling services from getting into the executive board room or abort initiatives before they have the opportunity to deliver on the promise.

What You'll Learn

You will learn the multiple potential benefits of seriously selling services and why most product companies should pursue this goal more aggressively. You will discover the research-based and field-proven core and best practices, lessons learned, and benchmarks for success. In addition, you'll learn what doesn't work, the common worst practices that hamper and sometimes kill selling services initiatives, and how to effectively avoid them or at least lessen their impact. Also, I'll share examples and make recommendations, that if implemented as suggested, will both speed and smooth your transition to seriously selling services.

Here are some of the key themes and core content that will be explored and explained in this book:

- The misconception that selling services lowers overall profit margins.
- Why selling services helps sell more products.
- How to determine if selling services is appropriate for your organization.
- Which of the three selling services strategies is right for you.
- What executives must say and do, and do again, to make the transition to selling services work.
- The common barriers to seriously selling services and the common steps taken to address these barriers that never work.
- Why getting the sales team to sell services is such a big deal.
- The five mandatory, have-to-do-it actions required to turn box pushers into sellers of the invisible.
- The four free-to-fee strategies that always fail.
- How to transition from free to fee and not irritate customers or drive the sales force crazy.
- Why everyone needs to sell services.
- How to tap the power of your hidden sales force within.
- How to grasp the challenge of the channel and adapt strategies that will work.
- The 10 steps to building a portfolio of services that customers want and will pay for.
- Why leaders of services organizations,are "strangers in a strange land."
- The five stages of leading services in a product company that are required both for organizational effectiveness and personal sanity.

Who Should Read This Book?

- Executives of product companies looking for more, profitable revenue and/or opportunities for competitive differentiation.

- Leaders of services organizations inside product companies trying to master the nuances of delivering optimum value both to customers and the business.
- Managers of selling organizations trying to sell more services and solutions.
- Marketers tasked with mastering services marketing to better support sales.
- Sellers of products, services, and solutions trying to meet and exceed their sales targets.
- Consultants, field engineers, technical support experts—everyone who touches the customer!
- Researchers attempting to gain a better understanding of the field realities of selling services within product companies.
- Internal practitioners (e.g., human resources, training, organization development, quality) desiring to do a better job with their internal customers.
- External practitioners (e.g., analysts, management consultants) attempting to do a better job with their clients.

Further Clarification

Services Not Service
This book is about selling services, not service. Yes, customer service is an important contributor to an organization's performance, and I value it highly. However, this book is about selling services as an offering ranging from service contracts to training to assessments to product maintenance to managed services to process improvement.

B2B (Business-to-Business) Product Companies
This book will provide practical, usable information for anyone tasked with selling or helping support the selling of services. However, its research base and experience focus is B2B product companies attempting to grow their services businesses. Special emphasis is put on the unique challenges that selling in that environment entails.

Organization Maturity
Note that some content is targeted specifically at starting up services capabilities, but most everything will be of value for those desiring to take services to the next level of performance whatever their existing place on the maturity/performance curve.

Caveat
Again, most all readers from B2B product companies will gain from using the concepts contained in these pages. However, the more complex the environment you operate in, the more important your offerings are to your customer, the more the investment your customers must make, then the higher the potential value of selling services is to your organization, the greater the potential value this book will present to its readers.

Readability
Throughout the book you'll find three types of "call-outs" designed to improve readability:
- Gist: The critical idea of the content.
- Ponder Point: A concept worth giving thought.
- Best Practice: An action proven highly effective in most situations.

A Final Word to the Reader

This book addresses an important topic that deserves serious attention. In fact, I've devoted many years of my life to learning the ins and outs of success. However, I've attempted to add a dash of humor and the occasional tongue-in-cheek comment to make the writing process more fun for me and the reading process a tad more enjoyable for you. Your tolerance is appreciated if my attempts at jocularity miss their intended mark!

CHAPTER 1

Services and the Big Picture

What role should services play in your company? Should services be thought of as a strategic differentiator or a tactical contributor? Should services be managed as a profit center or as a cost center? What should you be doing differently with services to improve the performance of your organization?

This chapter looks at services as it relates to the overall business strategy, and thus it is specifically geared toward the business executive who has responsibility for the overall success of the total business—where to focus and where to invest. Hence, it will target the big picture, and leave more tactical information for later. Where relevant, specific issues and themes mentioned here will be explored in greater depth in future chapters outlining steps to transitioning to selling services success.

In this chapter, you'll learn the many potential organizational benefits of seriously selling services, and discover which of the three selling services strategies is best for your company. You'll be introduced to the high-level transition process to make selling services happen and learn the obstacles unique to this type of change initiative. Finally, you'll find out the three big responsibilities that executives must assume and the five best practices that executives must implement to successfully drive and support the selling of more services.

Why Sell Services Anyway?

Sell More Initial Deals

Here is a bit of blasphemy: Most customers view your products as commodities! Regardless of how truly unique or elegant or innovative your products are from your perspective, in most all buying situations, customers see no meaningful difference in the top two or three products in any category, across all industries, across all geographies. Yes, I understand this may not be 100% factual, but from the perception of the customer it is true. Hence, the old adage comes into play: Perception is reality. Kind of a sobering thought.

Once customers have determined their short list of the two or three potential products or bundles of products that they will seriously consider buying, they almost always cast their product ballot based on what they believe are the best services that surround the product—services that will best ensure the product works as promised, keeps working, and does so with a minimum of hassle and added expense. It is important to note that, in many cases, they will pay a premium for your offering if they understand the higher value your services bring to them. In essence, they vote with their pocketbook.

Furthermore, if your salespeople were strategic and sold an assessment early in the buying process—before needs were clear and products were specified—the probability of you getting the product business later on is greatly improved, giving you the chance to shape the final recommendations early while building relationships with people key to the final purchase.

GIST: Selling services effectively from the get-go will land you more initial deals.

Handle Fewer Train Wrecks

Sadly, sometimes products are positioned to the customer with these words coming out of the salesperson's mouth: "Our products don't break. You don't need any additional services," or "It is so easy to implement our software. Just read the manual and you can do it, no worries." This is all a bunch of baloney, especially if you are dealing with a fairly complex situation, an important customer process, and/or the customer has little if any familiarity with the implementation. Rare is the product that will not need some type of service in its life cycle, whether a tailored implementation, ongoing maintenance, software updates, refurbishing, and on and on. Not positioning this reality of life with the customer upfront is negligent selling.

Services appropriately sold up front greatly improves the probability that:

- The product will work the way it is supposed to work the first time.
- Greater functionality of the product will be utilized.
- Irritated customers ringing the bell of the fire engine, escalating their concerns up your organization ladder, will be greatly minimized.

GIST: Selling services upfront saves your organization, time, hassle, and money over the long term.

Sell More Products and Services Later

Experience also shows that when deals are sold with services up front, more products and services are sold later on (Hahn, 2007). Services greatly improve the chances that installation and implementation will be done correctly the first time, and services and support improve uptime and productivity. Delivering services means dealing personally with customer personnel and, done properly, starts to build trust-based relationships. These customers are very likely to buy more of your products (and more services, of course) and are well on the way to being loyal, highly profitable customers for life.

Figure 1 shows a real-world example of this revenue opportunity beyond the initial product sale. By selling services correctly

Figure 1

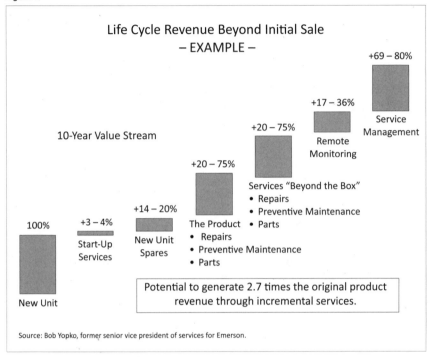

Source: Bob Yopko, former senior vice president of services for Emerson.

early on along with the product, this company had a very realistic opportunity to add 2.7 times the original product revenue through incremental services. In this example the product sold for approximately $100,000, so the potential for more services revenue was approximately $270,000. Plus, the customer was much more likely to buy this company's product at the end of the equipment's life.

GIST: Want to be a true total solutions provider? Services are the key.

Enjoy Predictable Revenue Streams
Want to see a CFO's eyes light up? Watch her face the first time she grasps an understanding of the predictable, repeatable sales that

come from a services business built upon service and support contracts coupled with a finely tuned professional services capability. This is pure joy to a bean counter. The services annuity stream makes life a whole lot easier for all of management, as it helps to take the guesswork out of business financials and becomes an early warning, leading indicator of organization success or failure.

> GIST: Strong services help you manage your business more effectively.

Differentiate Yourself

Depending on the maturity of your industry, your competitor's strategy, and your competitor's dealings with distribution, services can differentiate you in a really big way. The more complex your products, the more they cost the customer; and the more mission critical they are to your customer's business, the more the value-packing promise of services. Leading services researchers note from their studies that more and more companies in tough competitive markets are looking at services to yield competitive advantage (Brown, Gustafsson and Witell, 2009). If your competitors don't have full portfolios of strong service offerings or if they don't know how to sell them, this is a huge opportunity for you if you embrace the challenge. Give your customers what they need, want, and will pay for while locking out everyone else.

> GIST: Services are the drivers of market dominance.

Create New Markets

Business consultants like to talk about adjacency strategy (Zook, 2004), the strategy of building upon an organization's core competencies in one market to transport those capabilities to an adjacent, but different market space. For example, a company with specialized battery technology designed for the automotive industry could potentially attempt to build upon that battery expertise to develop and sell to the marine market. The same possibilities hold true with services. For example, an energy utilization assessment developed for the automotive industry could be adapted for the marine market. Taking advantage of your past experience and expertise can crack new markets and expand profitable revenue.

> GIST: Services adjacency strategy can be a powerful component of any growth blueprint.

To summarize, services have proven themselves to be able to contribute significant value to many, many product companies through profitable growth of both products and services. Properly executed, strong services capabilities can increase customer satisfaction and generate customer loyalty. In addition, for some companies, having the right portfolio of services helps smooth the entry into new markets. Finally, in some cases, having an arsenal of new or better services can create competitive differentiation.

> *Question:* But aren't services less profitable?
> *Answer:* Normally not.

Here are the core elements of a conversation I had with the CEO of a software company that I was interviewing as part of a services assessment for his company.

> *Alexander: Tell me what role you'd like services to play in helping your company be successful.*
> *CEO: Frankly, I wish services was a much smaller part of the*

business. They negatively impact our overall profitability. Every time I talk to financial analysts they beat me up on this issue. If you can tell me how to eliminate services altogether, I'd been extremely happy.

This perception is fairly common among executives at companies with high product profit margins. However, in most cases it is not entirely correct.

On average, my research shows that there is no difference between the profit margins of products and those of services.* In general, product profit margins have decreased as industries have matured, and services profit margins have increased as services management has learned how to optimize their organizations. For example, professional services organizations within product companies have improved their profitability by seven points over the last decade. In fact, top-performing services organizations have profit margins double that of their products.

There are exceptions, of course. New products in new industries could have higher profit margins initially. However, experience shows that product margins will consistently drop. A few products, due to their innovation or patents or special circumstances, may be able to maintain very high product margins over time.

Yet, recalling the high value that customers place on services, adding a portfolio of services, even at lower margins than products, will increase the overall value to the customer. Hence, looking at blended margins is probably a much more realistic way to view and understand overall profitability.

Finally, examining the financials of many services businesses inside product companies raises a few eyebrows, if not a few questions, about how profitability is calculated and the fairness of the calculations. Here are some issues to consider:

- If services consultants are spending 30% of their time in a presales role, why isn't that expense charged to sales?
- If you are a VAR (value-adding reseller) and your partner agreements require you to have a number of certified experts on staff,

shouldn't some of the costs of having these low-billable people on board be charged elsewhere?

- If a big customer has a blow-up, and company execs require a busload of the services business' top technical talent to do whatever it takes to fix the problem at no charge to the customer, should that cost be eaten by the services business?

My own biased experience says that if you sell the right services to the right customers in the right way, they will be very profitable and make the rest of your products look much better as well.

> GIST: Re-look and re-think cost allocation, pricing strategies, and margin expectations versus customer value. There is a good chance that you don't readily have this information, and it will take time to get the quality data you need.

What Must Executives Do to Successfully Drive and Support Selling More Services?

With all the potential benefits described above, why don't more product companies sell more services? There are several factors that can hinder or even stop this initiative in its tracks. Certain obstacles can be predicted to be a part of any significant change. These generic barriers to success will be reviewed, but only in general. However, there are several aspects unique to selling services that make this transition a tad more trying. These special challenges will be described in more detail, and strategies to overcome them will be provided.

Below is an executive-level view of the process for taking the selling of services within product companies to the next level of performance. Note that to be successful, the executive team must embrace and support all steps described to avoid the fits and starts of ad hoc change. Just like a set of religious tenets or commandments, all steps must be followed; this is not pick and choose.

Step One: Accept the Difficulty of the Task

Ponder Point: If it were easy, everybody would be doing it.

Let's face it, for most product companies, getting serious about aggressively building, marketing, and selling services is a big deal— a major change. The troubling truth of the matter is that about three out of four major change efforts fail to achieve and sustain the desired objectives (Alexander, 2004). My own experience in advising organizations confirms this, and your personal experiences probably do as well. Think back over the last few years during times when you experienced the launching of initiatives (e.g., implementing an ERP or CRM system, adapting Six Sigma, going "Lean"). How many of these efforts have brought about the lasting value intended at the time of announcement?

And anyone who has participated in an organizational change effort knows the tension that develops and the resistance that naturally occurs when the people of the organization are asked to behave in new and different ways. Productivity immediately drops as water-cooler conversations (both face-to-face and electronic) speculating on the impact and political ramifications of the change and the always-present "what's going to happen to me?" take a priority over the mundane tasks of meeting customer requirements. In addition to the obvious loss of focus and efficiency, other multiple "costs of resistance" take their toll, touching everything from loss of key employees to lowered corporate credibility to stifled innovation.

Understand the Obstacles to Any Change
Shortly, I will introduce the best practices of transitioning to a high-performance services organization inside a product company. However, before discussing what to do, it is important to ponder what not to do. Ten common obstacles that occur time and again when organizations and the people who compose them attempt to do things

Figure 2

Why Change Doesn't Produce Change

1. Not tied to strategy.
2. Seen as a fad or quick fix.
3. Short-term perspective.
4. Political realities undermine change.
5. Grandiose expectations versus simple successes.
6. Inflexible change designs.
7. Lack of leadership regarding change.
8. Lack of measurable results.
9. Fear of the unknown.
10. Inability to mobilize commitment to sustain change.

Source: Ulrich, David. 1996. *Human Resource Champions*. Harvard Business School Press.

differently are outlined in Figure 2.

Do you recognize any of them? I don't believe further elaboration is required. Needless to say, all must be recognized, and steps need to be put in place to deal with each of them. In addition to these 10 obstacles, there are some special challenges in transitioning to a seriously selling services business that must be considered before embarking on the journey of change.

Special Challenges of Transitioning to Services Selling

As already noted, big-time change targeted at making major improvements in organization performance is tough. Yet, making the transition to seriously selling services is often on a more difficult order of magnitude. Two factors drive this:

- *The Invisible Factor.* The first factor is the extreme difference between products and services. Products are tangible; they can be seen, felt, and easily quantified. However, services are intangible; they are invisible to the producer, the seller, and the customer. Evert Gummesson, a services researcher, probably said it the most eloquently: "Services are something that can be bought and sold but can't be dropped on your foot." The challenge of dealing with the added complexity of intangibility alone raises the bar. In addition, some other major differences between the

Figure 3

Offering Comparison: Products versus Services

PRODUCTS	SERVICES
Products are produced.	Services are performed.
The goal of producing products is uniformity.	The goal of performing services is uniqueness.
The customer is not involved in production.	The customer often is involved in the service performance.
Internal quality control compares outputs to specifications. If improperly produced, the product can be recalled.	Customers conduct quality control by comparing expectations to specifications. If improperly performed, apologies and reparation are the only means of recourse.
The morale and skill of the production workers is important.	The morale and skill of service providers is critical.

Source: Adapted from Alexander, James A. 1996. "Marketing Products with Services and Knowledge." *The Professional Journal*. Fort Myers, FL: AFSMI.

two types of offerings, as shown in Figure 3, are worth noting.

These distinctions have a fundamental impact on how one produces, markets, sells, delivers, services, and measures the performance of services offerings and the success of the services organization itself. What may have worked extremely well in managing a traditional product company often will be ineffective in running the services component. Hence, different characteristics and competencies in people must be sought, different management support systems must be created, and different metrics to reward performance and guide the enterprise must be developed. For example, even if all the recommendations in this book are followed, an estimated one-third of your product sellers will never be successful selling services! This is a significant management challenge. Later chapters will discuss this in detail and outline how to deal with these obstacles.

- *The Culture Fights Back Factor.* The second critical factor is the significance of dealing with organization culture. Any manager who has been around for a few years understands the power of the company culture to resist change, even change that is necessary for survival. The culture will do whatever it can to maintain the status quo. Aggressively selling services in a product-thinking, product-acting business is a full frontal attack on the existing culture, and the defensive mechanisms of the organization will resist any way it can. The fundamental problem is that, in most cases, the people running the show got there by being exceptionally good at making, marketing, and selling products. Products are their expertise, and this expertise got them promoted. Their past successes built around products helped create, develop, and nurture the culture—a culture that lives, breathes, and reinforces products-related success while shunning other alternatives to business. In this setting, services were regarded as necessary evils that were tolerated because they were a requirement in supporting products. Service was traditionally a cost center, and services were things negotiated and often given away either to make a sale or to keep a customer happy.

My services research, shown in Figure 4, confirms the critical importance of understanding and addressing the product company culture. As you see, culture change dwarfs all the other obstacles that must be dealt with for a product company to be successful in building and selling services.

Seriously selling services requires a serious change in thinking about the business. Services now must be viewed as an equal offering of the organization, a true value-adder, the potential differentiator in the marketplace, and an important contributor to profitable revenue. Executives now must view products as customers have for a long time—as commodities that take a secondary role in a total solutions package. Services management and services employees must now vie for the respect that they may not have held before. This is not an easy transition to make, as it flies directly in the face of the tried and true.

Furthermore, certain departments are more threatened than

Figure 4

Biggest Challenge

What was (or is) the single most significant challenge your organization faced (or is facing) in building and selling services?

58%	**Culture Change**	4%	Obtaining Funding
8%	Acquiring Capabilities	4%	Intra-Service Conflict
7%	Selling	2%	Project Management
6%	Marketing	1%	Retaining Employees
5%	Senior Management Commitment		

Source: Alexander, James A. 2004. *The State of Professional Services II: An Industry Comes of Age.* St. James City, FL: Alexander Consulting.

---

others, as different internal groups, possibly product marketing or engineering, for example, feel that making services more important makes them less important. Transitioning to a more services-friendly, services-are-good-for-our-business mindset confronts internal tradition, established ways of thinking, and embedded power that will work together to try and squelch the selling of services.

Often it is true that the very things that made you successful yesterday are the same things that hinder your success today. Bringing about this services business mind shift is a leadership challenge of the highest order.

> GIST: Set the compass heading to north, then stay the course, constantly bringing back the needle in the face of high seas, stiff winds, and changing currents.

Step Two: Align the Services Strategy with the Business Mission

Ponder Point: Stuff rolls downhill.

As in any business, if you don't get the strategy right, it is darn near impossible to get the marketing right, the selling right, or anything else right—stuff rolls downhill.

My research in the technology industry confirms this criticality and expands it to the realities of being embedded inside a product company. A key differentiator that separates top-performing services organizations within product companies from everybody else is their ability to better align their strategy with the mission and focus of the parent organization. Of course this makes perfect sense, but doing so is a constant challenge.

The repercussions of non-alignment can be quite severe, as there is nothing worse than doing things really well that shouldn't be done in the first place. For example, maximizing utilization rates can be an important target of a mature, free-standing professional services organization (PSO), but if the appropriate strategy of a PSO is primarily that of supporting the parent company by helping to sell products, the goals may be in conflict to the overall detriment of the company. As the quality folks say, "optimizing one group [the PSO in this case] while sub-optimizing the organization."

Strategic alignment means determining which of three possible strategic roles of services best supports the overall business mission. Take a look at it from your perspective. Which phrase best describes your company today?

1. *Product-enablement.* The purpose of the services organization is to make sure that the product works as intended.
2. *Product-enhancement.* Along with product enablement, the services organization is expanded to contribute to profitable revenue by providing additional value-adding services that impact customer functionality, process effectiveness, and efficiency.
3. *Services-led.* The company pushes services and pulls products.

Figure 5 shows that about 15% of technology services organizations within product companies assume the role of product enablement, 75% are product enhancers, and 10% fall into the category of services-led (Alexander, 2007).

Number one, product enablement, is pretty straightforward. The role of services is to support the product, help get the business in

Figure 5

Source: Alexander, James, A. 2002. *The State of S-Business: An International Study of Progress, Performance and Best Practices.* Ft. Myers, FL: AFSMI.

pre-sales, help keep the business through successful installation (or implementation or commissioning or start up), and troubleshoot, where needed. Products have been, are, and will be the dominant focus. Enough said.

Number three, services-led, is also easy to understand, as the organization pushes the benefits of services and services-led solutions first, and then pulls along their products. Here we emphasize development of new and unique services offerings, encourage the sales folks (and everyone) to sell services, and manage utilization.

Number two, product enhancement, is the tricky one, being betwixt and between, neither fish nor fowl. In this strategy, senior management wants to have its cake and eat it too. This is a philosophy I admire! However, this is not easy to do. Let me give you an example of the pressure this strategy puts on the services organization. This is a summary of what I often hear from services vice presidents far too often that really exemplifies this challenge:

> *On Monday I had my review with the CEO, and she assured me that my mission was to support the company by profitably growing services revenue while keeping our customers happy. This was just what I wanted to hear! On Tuesday the vice president of sales stopped by, really concerned about services pricing and the need*

to 'value-price' (code word 'deep discount') services to help land strategic business. I laid out my best defense—my mandate to drive business, the need for the sales force to really sell value—but in the end I lost the discussion as I knew I would. Sales trumps services every time. My profit margins just took a hit. Bummer.

Then on Wednesday morning I was called into a crisis meeting and ordered by the CEO (the same person I talked with Monday) to board a Boeing to Boston with my best technical experts to fix the problems at Galactic Enterprises and not to come back until the client was satisfied. Never mind that my people were committed to other projects, and of course, it wasn't billable; it was for the 'good of the company.' Forget about what was said, this is a product company first. I just have to live with it and try and make my numbers any way I can.

Figure 6 shows that each services strategy requires different philosophies for success. Running a product-enablement business requires constant vigilance toward efficiency. Hence, the entire services organization is focused on keeping things lean and low cost. Implementing a product-enhancement strategy requires a focus on effectiveness—balancing the requirements of profitable growth with the necessity of helping to sell products on one hand, and keeping

Figure 6

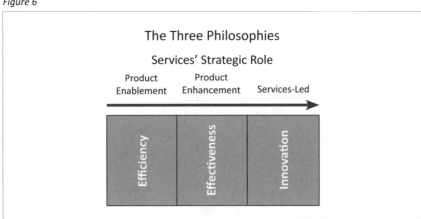

customers satisfied on the other hand. Constant negotiations with sales and other executives are required to deliver on the duality of expectations. Running services in a services-led organization requires emphasis on innovation, as the services component is recognized as the greatest potential value contributor. Emphasis is on the creation of unique services that differentiate the organization from the competition. Marketing and selling push services and pull along the products.

Obviously, each philosophy requires different capabilities and mindsets to optimize performance. So being absolutely, positively sure of the strategic role of your services organization is vital to running it appropriately.

GIST: Do it right the first time—conduct a strategic alignment assessment where you consider how services can best contribute to organization success balanced against your existing capabilities, your customer issues and needs, and your competitive position. This is too important to the future of the organization not to get it right. Confirm your services strategic role today, and get the facts to demonstrate what the role needs to be in two years. This can be done quickly and economically, and the benefits can be huge:

- Base decisions on facts, not best guesses.
- Align your services with the practices and processes most appropriate for your strategy.
- Focus on the realistic, not the wishful.
- Involve senior management and other team members in the process to develop momentum for future changes.
- Benchmark your performance against others to monitor your success.
- Save yourself headaches and hassle.

Once you've got the strategy right, it's time to take a serious look at your commitment.

Step Three: Go Big or Stay Home

Here my bias shows through once again, but I've seen a group of top management review, discuss, and approve tens of millions of dollars for new plants all within a single 30-minute meeting. I've also seen this same group of executives agonize over the course of several meetings and several months over spending $60,000 to launch a pilot services project that would validate the services assumptions and business model that all agree is vital to long-term business success. Amazing when you first think about it, but remember the backgrounds of these executives. They have grown up in products and have been successful because of their knowledge learned running product companies. They have the experience and the insights to make competent, correct product decisions quickly and confidently. However, as pointed out, services are a different business, and as any of us would do when faced with something out of our expertise, the tendency is to cautiously go slow and keep a very tight rein on funding.

Yes, you should look for low-hanging fruit that doesn't take large investments, and target quick wins to help pay your costs. If there are doubts about the value of services within your organization, then conducting a pilot is a low-investment, low-risk way to confirm your services assumption and demonstrate its value.

Please resist the temptation to cautiously cut corners in hope that magically a new business will sprout and bloom without adequate fertilizer, water, and grooming. Don't do it. Anything in life worth having requires a commitment of time, money, focus, and sweat. Remember, you are creating a new business! If your senior management group is not willing to invest to build a services capability the right way, then save your energy for better times. As Lou Gerstner, past chairman and CEO of IBM, said in his book, *Who Says Elephants Can't Dance*:

In building services, there's no such thing as a toe in the water. When you take this plunge, it's full-body immersion...I've said repeatedly that this is the kind of capability you can't simply acquire (though our competitors keep trying). The bet you're really making is on your own commitment to invest both the years and the capital, then build the experience and discipline it takes to succeed.

GIST: In for a penny, in for a pound.

Hopefully, I've made my point. There are many obstacles that can cause a selling services initiative to stumble, and like any meaningful change, it takes stalwart executive support to make it successful.

If you have any serious hesitation now, don't launch the selling services initiative—you will do more harm than good. Remember: In for a penny, in for a pound.

Best Practices

Finally, here are some proven best practices of executives that have successfully guided the transition to seriously selling services:

1. *Create a sense of urgency.* When people are reluctant to do something, they will come up with every excuse imaginable to put it off. Change is time-sensitive, and prolonged hesitation only makes things more difficult. Leadership is needed to trumpet the cause and build the emotional momentum needed to break the status quo and get things rolling. To demonstrate urgency and show your seriousness, initially host highly visible weekly updates on progress. Personally call and write people to ask how it is going. Put this at the top of your to-do list each day. Publically publish selling services success performance so that everyone can see progress. To emphasize the criticality, publish results versus targets not only quarterly, but monthly, weekly, even daily. Break it down by division, geography, even by salesperson in order to build the necessary momentum of change. Remember that when you are challenging the status quo, fast is better than slow.

2. *Tie executive compensation to seriously selling services success.* Make seriously selling services a core objective tied to compensation for the entire executive team. Yes, you "get it," but your executive colleagues may not. These are the same people who achieved their success and power through the very system you are trying to alter dramatically. Remember that it is rare for the ruling class to support the revolutionaries, so the case for change must be seen as the only choice for organizational survival. Everyone will be watching for the slightest wavering at the top to justify stalling or just plain non-compliance, and the best way to prevent this is a one-for-all-and-all-for-one approach to compensation based upon hard numbers and firm time frames.

3. *Make heroes out of those who attempt the change.* As I'll discuss in greater detail later, this is a scary change for many people, and you want to look for every opportunity to reinforce their new, seriously selling services behavior, even when the results aren't as good as you like. Make it a point of singling out those who are doing what you request of them at your weekly feedback sessions. Send them notes and copy everyone, publish their success in internal newsletters and magazines, and give them small incentives to keep them going. Early on, it is the little things that matter.

4. *Give zero tolerance for slackers.* Here is the scenario: It is year end, and overall you have made good progress with selling services. However, your top seller, Ace Flanagan, has blown the doors off his product quota, doubling his target and selling twice as much product as anyone else. However, Ace didn't come close to reaching his services quota, ending up at 28%. Your vice president of sales doesn't want to rock the boat and risk losing Ace, so he suggests business as usual, paying Ace full commission and bonuses.

    What a great opportunity! After telling your vice president of sales thanks but no thanks, you have a one-on-one sit down with Ace. First you thank him for his product sales contribution, but then quickly state your major disappointment in his services performance. You confirm that this is the new strategy, it is vital to the company, and that everyone is expected to contribute. You are sorry, but he will not get any bonus, he and his wife will not be going to Bora-Bora as part of the President's Circle, and if he misses his quota next year, he will be fired.

5. *Stay the course.* There is a good probability that 90 to 120 days into the transition to seriously selling services that performance will actually go down. If you are doing the right things, giving lots of training, involving people in the process, and allowing for the inevitable lost water-cooler time, overall sales could well drop. Anticipated services sales may not materialize as people try to figure out how to do it, and product sales will drop due to lost time out of the field and the lowered productivity that comes with the deer-in-headlights stare when people are passively aggressive.

Don't panic! If you give up now you will never get services off the ground and you most likely will never regain your level of past product sales. Suck it up, stand tall, damn the torpedoes, full speed ahead!

Conclusion

Managing the transition to seriously selling services has an immense upside for most companies. New, profitable revenue streams, more sales of products, higher levels of customer satisfaction, and competitive differentiation are all probable outcomes of a well-executed shift to services. Know that the path to services success is clear and the obstacles are well-known.

As with any significant change, strong leadership is a critical success component. A services leadership framework exists, and executives willing to listen to the voice of those who already have made the journey will enjoy major rewards in a relatively short period of time. For most organizations, the time for seriously selling services is now!

CHAPTER 2

Turning Box Pushers into Sellers of the Invisible

How do you get your product sellers to quit discounting or giving away services?

This chapter answers this critical yet difficult question. You will learn what you need to do to get salespeople who view services as giveaways—to be thrown in any way and any time in order to get the product business—to actively, consistently sell the value of the services you offer.

First, however, you'll learn what not to do—the common mistakes that lead to failure or, at the very least, greatly slow down the progress of getting your product sellers to successfully sell services. You'll find out why what seems to be appropriate doesn't work. Then you'll be introduced to the five "gotta do" steps for making this transformation effective.

Be prepared: Some of your product sellers won't make this transition; that's a fact. However, if you judiciously follow the steps outlined in this chapter, two out of three product salespeople can make the shift to successfully selling services.

Common Approaches That Just Don't Work

Here's the scenario: Senior management has bought into seriously selling services and wants to get moving on it. When advised by a services expert that selling services is "way different" from selling products and requires special actions to succeed, they respond that they have a good sales force, and a good sales force can sell anything—just tell them what to do and back it up with solid incentives. They decide to kick off this initiative at the annual sales conference. See if this situation strikes a chord:

The Big Boss strides toward the podium and gazes out upon the entire sales force huddled in the banquet hall, awaiting word on the new launch. The Big Boss soberly rolls into the presentation, banging the drum of doom about lackluster performance, the challenges of the marketplace, and the potential wrath of stockholders if things continue as is. The figures formulated by the consulting firm hired to build this case spell out the problems (in PowerPoint, naturally) in cold, hard figures. The message is clear: Sell more, better and faster—change or die.

But just as quickly, the atmosphere changes. The Big Boss dramatically stops the presentation and smiles broadly at the audience. Then, on cue and as if choreographed by a TV producer (it probably was), the balloons drop and the band begins playing something like "Back in the High Life Again." (Note that if the meeting is in Las Vegas, live animals come on stage.) Next, animated slides (yes, more PowerPoint) proclaim the dawn of a new era, the Golden Age of "Total Value Solutions" (or something like that—they all sound the same, don't they?). TVS, as it is quickly dubbed, will be the touchstone, the compass, the blueprint for trekking the treacherous path from the abyss and leading the company back to its former greatness and beyond. As the four-color glossy listing the new expectations of the sales force and the new compensation program is passed out to everyone in the hall, sellers are asked to stand up and swear their personal allegiance to the "Six Selling Steps to TVS."

On the outside, the salespeople smile broadly, nod their heads, and quickly start using new TVS catch words, enthusiastically applauding the visionary leadership at the front of the room. Ace Flanagan, the company's top product seller starts a standing ovation.

On the inside, the salespeople are quickly doing two things. First, they do the math on the new compensation program. Their rough calculations show that even the big percentage spiff on selling services is small potatoes when looking at total compensation. Yes, it would be nice to make a few extra bucks, but it is probably not worth the effort. Second, they are weighing the seriousness of what is being said. If you meet your product quota, no one will slap your wrist for not making your services number, will they? This is a product company, right? Besides, this looks like just another Program-of-the-Month. The salespeople decide to talk the talk and wave the flag when asked, but keep a low profile and do business as usual. "This too shall pass" becomes their unspoken mantra.

Fast-Forward

As the year goes by, an obviously frustrated senior management continues to beat the drum of TVS, but sales of services hardly improve at all. Extra bonuses are promised, threats are made, but at year-end nothing much has changed, and the promise of selling services is lost. The grandiose launch has been a total failure. Furthermore, senior management has lost some credibility, while the product-is-everything culture has been solidified even more. What was supposed to be a game-changing venture ended up being the Flavor-of-the-Season that sales accurately anticipated.

What went wrong? In a perfect world, all of us in business would behave altruistically, taking care of the customer first, the company second, and finally, our own needs. The business case for seriously selling services is strong. But in reality, that's not the way it works. Although everyone may cross their heart, swear allegiance, and drink the Kool-Aid at the global kickoff, it will take much more than that to change selling behavior.

Salespeople, indeed all of us, behave in ways within some ethical boundary that maximize personal gain as easily as possible with a minimum of hassle and stress. This is not a question of values, but a fact of life. I know, I know, there are cultural and situational factors that impact the degree to which altruism is practiced, but it is a reality nonetheless.

For example, in organizations that primarily reward sellers on gross sales, sellers are highly motivated to do whatever it takes to sell the product at the possible expense of everything else. So would you if your desired lifestyle depended on it. If they don't sell services, oh well. If they give away services, big deal. Getting the product sale is the prime consideration. Why should they change? For the good of the services organization? Forget it. For the good of the company? No way!

GIST: If you want to change selling behavior (in this case, selling services and not giving them away), you must address all the factors that impact seller motivation.

Steps to Selling Services Success

Here are the steps to make this happen:

Step One: Remove Excuses
Most salespeople weaned on selling products say that selling services:
- Lengthens the sales cycle, thus jeopardizing their 30- and 90-day numbers.
- Raises the overall price, thus making the deal more susceptible to competitors.
- Lowers their income potential because, compared to the price of products, services are small change, and time spent on services takes away more valuable time spent on products.
- In addition, most product salespeople will not say it, but they

feel that selling services challenges their abilities, as it is much different than selling products and, actually, a little scary.

> GIST: Now, is it any wonder why services and solutions sales performance is so poor?

However, these stated reasons are not correct. Let's review each of these assumptions from the viewpoint of serious services sellers — those who truly understand it:

- *Lengthens the selling cycle, thus jeopardizing their 30- and 90-day numbers.* **False.** Top sellers understand that services are a vital part of the customer's value proposition and need to be sold with the product at the time of the product sale. Furthermore, when selling complex solutions, selling some services up-front (e.g., an assessment or audit) can actually compress the overall solution selling cycle.
- *Raises the overall price, thus making the deal more susceptible to competitors.* **True and False.** Of course the overall dollar amount increases when more offerings are provided. However, properly done, the value potential of a true solution increases dramatically. As your organization performs services, credibility and trust rise, lowering the possibilities of competitive inroads.
- *Lowers their income potential because, compared to the price of products, services are small change.* **Really False.** When your selling arsenal only includes products, you are quickly viewed as a commodity seller, where price becomes the customer's hammer and you become the nail. Your percentage of wins goes down, and you are totally susceptible to competitors who know how to sell services and solutions. When you sell solutions, both your deal size and your win rate increase.
- *Challenges their abilities, as it is much different than selling products and, actually, a little scary.* **True.** Selling services and solutions effectively is different, more difficult, and initially frustrating to

those used to transaction selling. Top sellers understand this, accept it, and do whatever it takes to improve their capabilities; it is as much an attitude as it is a set of skills.

Whether product sellers actually believe these points or just use them as company-acceptable excuses, they must be addressed head-on. So find the figures that demonstrate that services can be sold. Use respected companies that successfully sell lots of services as proof, compare your results with what your competitors have done, and present research showing that customers value services and want to buy them. This information is readily available, so use it.

Furthermore, several of the steps listed below also address these excuses and reinforce the message that, when properly done, selling services is good for everyone.

Step Two: Align the System with the Strategy

Adjust your sales performance management system (objectives, tools, rewards, consequences, and feedback) to align with your new services selling strategy. Figure 7 shows the core elements of performance management and how they link together.

A. *Fitting performance specifications.* First, make it crystal clear that selling services is now an important focus of the company and an important required responsibility of the sales force. These expectations should be translated into quantifiable services sales goals (how much, what type, when) and should be in place and outlined in all sellers' quotas and in their performance plan.

B. *Adequate resources.* You must have the necessary knowledge, skills, and tools supported by quick and easy access to your knowledge management system and internal experts. Most of this is best introduced through training, as discussed below.

C. *Minimal interference.* In all probability, you have just added more responsibility and more work to your sellers, but have not taken away any of their product sales quotas. To give your sellers the time to learn and practice how to sell services in the field, you need to minimize or eliminate secondary expectations. For ex-

Figure 7

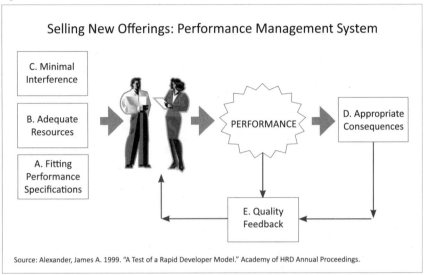

Selling New Offerings: Performance Management System

C. Minimal Interference

B. Adequate Resources

A. Fitting Performance Specifications

PERFORMANCE

D. Appropriate Consequences

E. Quality Feedback

Source: Alexander, James A. 1999. "A Test of a Rapid Developer Model." Academy of HRD Annual Proceedings.

ample, for the first six months, ask the marketing department to eliminate all requests of the sales force, minimize the amount of time you expect sellers to take executives around to visit customers—unless those visits include services sales coaching by the executive—try to hold off involving your salespeople in task forces, and reduce required paperwork and all the other things that keep them out of the field selling services along with products. Minimizing interference will not only free up time for your sellers to learn how to better sell services, it also will take away excuses for non-performance.

D. *Appropriate consequences.* First, add a carrot—link the achievement of services targets to lucrative incentives. You can scale back later. In an attempt to get the attention of your sales force, make sure you are paying a higher percentage of bonus on services compared to products. In addition, tack on some highly visible bonuses (five-day cruise for two, twin Harleys, country club memberships—whatever gets their interest) to generate some excitement when your box sellers make good services sales. Your best sellers like to compete among themselves, and this is a highly visible way to do it. If you really want to generate maximum interest in selling services, make sure the spouses are aware of the incentive program. They can apply pressure that sales management can never match.

Second, add a stick—put negative consequences in place if services selling goals are not met (no trip to the Bahamas for the services slackers, no product bonuses if services sales goals are not achieved). Punishment is a strong word, but necessary nonetheless. If your top product seller, Ace Flanagan, does poorly at selling services, put him on probation and let him know that job security requires services sales maturity. You will be sending a strong signal.

E. *Quality feedback.* The faster you get reliable performance feedback to people, the more likely they will self-direct their behavior to meet expectations and gain the positive incentives. Ideally, your sellers should be able to access their performance-to-goal anywhere, anytime. And, of course, management attention, encouragement, and coaching will increase the probability of repeatable, sustainable performance. Start every sales meeting with the selling services review of performance to demonstrate its importance and generate motivation.

The above process seems logical, doesn't it? These are classic, proven steps of how to change people performance. Yet I rarely see organizations that address all of these points from the start. Most executives will set services targets and provide solid incentives, then expect/hope/demand that selling behavior changes. It will not. The gap is too large, and the change is too scary. Without meaningful ramifications for not selling services, you are wasting your time. The result will be dismal (if any) increases in services sales and a year of frustration for management.

The important thing to remember here is to do all of these steps, or don't do them at all. But often management is very reluctant to put negative consequences in place around not selling services. (Maybe all the sellers will revolt!) Even if they put the negative consequences

in place, it takes a steel-backed sales executive to keep the top-pro-
ducing product seller (and his or her spouse) from making the trip
to Rio for not selling enough services. (Maybe he will quit!) Finally,
most product sellers, no matter how effective they are in that role,
find it hard to transition to selling the invisible. (Maybe they will just
fade away!)

GIST: Let me repeat: Getting the sales force to attempt to sell
services is only effective when:
- Objectives and metrics requiring them to sell services are a
  part of the selling package.
- Lucrative incentives are in place for selling services.
- There are meaningful negative consequences if their selling
  services objectives are not met.
- Management actually enforces the significant negative
  consequences if selling services objectives are not met.
- If you put a gun to their head, the sellers could effectively
  sell services on their own.

This is a nice segue to the next step, as once they are willing, they
must be able.

Step Three: Tailor Your Training
Invest in quality, services-specific sales training tailored to the issues and uniqueness of your situation. Generic, off-the-shelf packages have their place. SPIN Selling, Professional Selling Skills, and
Strategic Selling are all good basic primers for box sellers, but they
don't cut the mustard when selling the invisible. The mindset, approach, knowledge, skills, and tools are different when selling services. Therefore, you need to put everybody through high-quality,
services-specific sales training. Find services experts with training
competence and tailor a program specific to the needs of your organization. Make certain that the following components are part

of the curriculum: why sell services, how to sell intangibles, selling how customers want to buy, building trust, qualifying great services business, developing services power maps, selling services to the "C" level, compressing sales cycle time, and so forth. To keep things interesting and fun, incorporate lots of opportunity for participation, including custom role-plays built around specific scenarios that the sellers must address. It is important to get your product sellers both competent in their selling services capabilities and confident enough that they will try it with customers and prospects.

An important part of any good training is providing usable tools and teaching participants how to use them. Appropriate tools for selling services include feature-benefit profiles for all your key services offerings, qualifying checklists, case studies of customers espousing the value of using your services, ROI calculators, and sales call planners.

To maximize buy-in to a probably skeptical group, when I develop selling services training I like to involve the top product salespeople, the Ace Flanagans, in the development of the course. I use one-on-one interviews to understand their thinking. I also conduct focus groups with my client's best and average box sellers to understand their issues and challenges. I always interview sales management to learn their perspectives and their issues. Their participation will not only improve content quality, but also help gain needed credibility for the training. Even better, when possible I conduct interviews of key people within my client's key customers to learn their issues, expectations, wants, and needs regarding services, and then I build this into the training. This is an extremely powerful way to drive change, as it is fairly easy to dismiss your own views as biased, but it is difficult not to pay attention when your best customers say they want to buy services! See Chapter 5 on how to do it.

GIST: Remember this rule of change management: Those that contribute tend to support.

Step Four: Reinforce, Reinforce, Reinforce

Very strong training as outlined above is a vital catalyst, and is a mandatory start for changing selling behavior. Remember, though, for almost all of your sellers, this is a very big change, and training won't do it alone. Behavior change takes time and support, so be prepared to invest some time and money into it. Instead of thinking about a single two- or three-day training event, craft a learning system with ongoing reinforcement over at least a year (Figure 8).

For example, back up the core sales training with a reinforcement workshop within 90 days to let people share successes and practice new skills in a safe environment. Make sure that the date is announced during the core training, and that expectations for the reinforcement workshop are laid out for all participants. Just letting them know that they are to report on the usage of what they will be learning is a powerful motivator. An even more powerful incentive to get them to do what you ask of them is that they don't want to look stupid to their peers. This will greatly improve the odds of them paying attention and taking the training seriously. If you can't

Figure 8

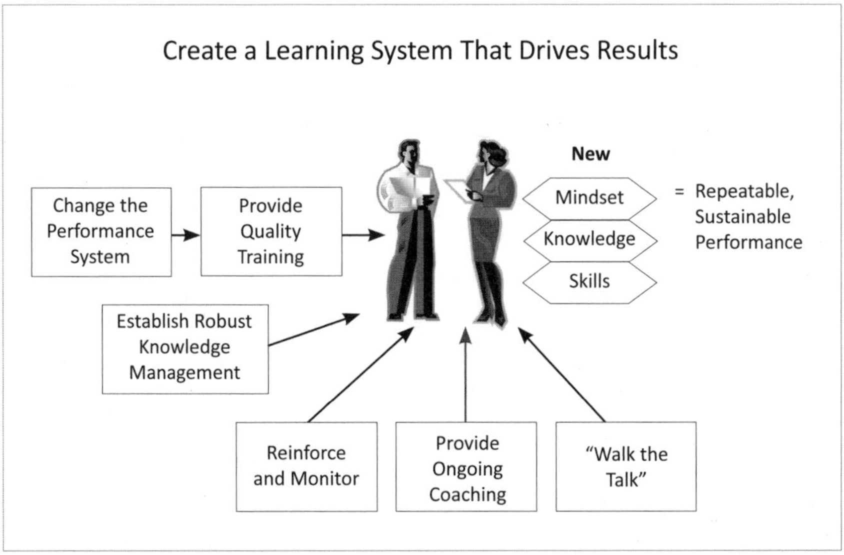

Create a Learning System That Drives Results

do a face-to-face reinforcement workshop, at least have a reinforcement video teleconference with the same objectives. Though obviously not as powerful as a face-to-face event, a couple hours of a well-facilitated session will still send a strong signal and advance the selling services cause. If you don't have video capabilities, then an old-fashioned Webinar can do the trick.

Also, make an electronic classroom available to allow for "ask the expert" dialogue and the further sharing of war stories. Participants may not want to "look dumb" to their management, but if trust was developed with the facilitator during the initial training, sellers will be more open to shoot straight and thus get the help they need to improve.

Consider investing money in providing in-field coaching. You are asking salespeople to perform much differently than they have in the past, and providing one-on-one modeling with real customers and coaching afterward are powerful motivators to personal change. In organizations where sales managers are responsible for hands-on coaching of their people and spend most of their time working with their sales reps, it makes sense to extend their skill set to coaching their people on selling services.

Note, however, that there are a couple of challenges to this approach. First, product sales managers within your company may not be much good at selling services either! Unless they have a different background than their sellers, they probably don't have the right knowledge, skills, and mindsets to coach the selling of services. Before sending them out to coach sellers on how to sell services, they will need to acquire not only the core training provided to the sales force, but additional training in how to coach. Again, this is another investment, but one that will pay off in the long run.

A second consideration is that in some companies "sales management" spends very little time actively managing salespeople. In these companies, sales managers are often the company's best sellers and have revenue targets of their own. These individuals are key to the company making its numbers. In these situations it is unrealistic to expect that they will be able to provide the reinforcement requirements outlined above. Not that they are lazy or evil, these folks have big bogies to make if they are to be successful, and that trumps people development every time. For example, I have a long-term client that has built his organization's success by having a very entrepreneurial approach to selling. The sales managers are the top sellers, and it is in the best interest of the company that they spend a minimum of 90% of their time in front of their customers. They contract me to do in-field coaching of their new hires to help accelerate their learning curve and speed their success. If your company follows this model then you should also look for outside expertise to do the one-on-one, in the trenches, customer-facing sales coaching needed to accelerate selling services performance.

> GIST: Behavioral change is difficult, and no matter how good the training is, you won't get the results you want without strong reinforcement.

Step Five: Realize the Reality
As mentioned in Chapter 1, it is important to stay the course. Things may get worse before they get better; overall sales volume may dip before it goes up. People will complain and look for every possible reason why this selling services thing is a terrible idea. You will need to stick to your guns as people test how serious you are. It is hard to do, but again, firing your number one box seller, Ace Flanagan, when he refuses to try and sell services sends a powerful message.

The other critical fact is that understanding and articulating the invisible is much more challenging than discussing feeds and speeds, features and functions. What you think, what you say, and what you do are different when selling services.

A few people adapt quickly and intuitively, most people, over time, can be adequate at selling intangibles given enough training, tools, and reinforcement, but another group will never quite get it. Not because they are bad people or don't try, but because they are wired differently. From a sales management perspective, this is a very big deal.

> GIST: Even if you follow all of this advice exactly as outlined, and I hope you do, about one in three product salespeople will not be successful in selling services. (Hey, it's not their fault—they were hired to sell boxes.) You should understand this from the beginning and be prepared to help them find new jobs inside or outside the company.

Conclusion

Getting the sales force to effectively sell services is critical to long-term success in seriously selling services. Sadly, the common approaches most executives take to bring about this change just don't work. To be effective, all aspects of the sales performance system must be changed, coupled with solid training, backed by strong reinforcement, and supported by a leadership team willing to make some tough calls to make sure that the change sticks.

It takes at least a year to yield meaningful results and often three years to make them effective. Yet, do not despair. The next chapter outlines the steps to kick-start selling services by getting everyone who touches the customer involved in the selling services process.

CHAPTER 3

Everybody Sells Services!

If it takes a year or more to get the product sales force effectively selling services, what can you do in the meantime to generate results? Most executives can't wait that long!

Relying entirely on the product sales force to drive services is not a good idea. In this chapter you will learn several things you can do to kick-start seriously selling services. You will discover how to tap into your hidden sales force—what it takes to get your technical talent competent, confident, and committed to seriously selling services. You will find out how to utilize other resources already in your organization (technical management, geographic or practice managers, executives) to help you drive services business. You'll also learn why many organizations would benefit from hiring or building dedicated services sellers. Finally, you will find out the potential benefits and challenges of team selling services by pairing up the product salesperson with pre-sales engineers or with dedicated services sellers or other technical talent.

Everybody Sells Everything

The title of this chapter, everybody sells services, is a vital component of ensuring that the transition works. In fact, it is a best practice of those who succeed. However, it is a subset of a larger business principle: Everybody sells everything. The concept is simple: Everyone who has contact with the customer (or prospects or partners or suppliers or the media or anyone) understands that a part of their job responsibility is to "sell" their organization, its capabilities, and the offerings it provides—the receptionist who makes everyone feel comfortable and welcome, the technical support specialist who doesn't treat you like an idiot and really cares about your problem, the finance person who takes the time to understand your needs and demonstrates a little flexibility. Organizations that embed this philosophy into their culture stand head and shoulders above their competitors.

Unleash Your Hidden Sales Force

Ponder Point: Trust drives sales, and those with the most customer trust are usually your technical talent.

There is no faster and easier way to grow profitable services revenue than by using your technical people to help sell your offerings. Nothing works better or quicker.

Why Is Using Technical Talent to Sell Such a Good Thing?

My research shows that a best practice of top services organizations within product companies is that their technical talent demonstrate appropriate selling skills. Let's look a little deeper to see why this is so powerful.

1. *There are lots of them.* Depending on the type of services sold and the services strategy, services providers usually outnumber salespeople. Of course it varies, but often the ratio is 20 to 1 or more—professional services consultants implementing projects, field services engineers doing preventive maintenance, technical support engineers resolving problems. Just think of the power of increasing your services selling capabilities if you can tap into just a part of this potential.

2. *They know the customer.* Services providers are where the action is. Who better understands the issues and day-to-day realities of customers than the folks who implement, prevent, troubleshoot, fix problems, and advise on new opportunities than a service technician who is in the building or on the phone every day and knows everyone from the facilities manager to the department head to the CIO? As they walk the plant floor or office hallways, eat in the lunchroom, and meet with technical staff, they become privy to a wealth of information specific to company issues, challenges, problems, and opportunities.

3. *They have established trust with the customer.* Trust is, of course, a main driver in decision making, and your technical talent often have a high level of customer trust, established from a history and track record of doing what they say they will do. When your technical people make suggestions, customers listen.

4. *They are not a threat.* Technical folks don't have "sales" on their business card. The "BS warning signal" that automatically goes off inside customers' heads when they come in contact with a salesperson does not sound when dealing with a technical person. Customers are much more likely to share their reality and respond to recommendations from a technical person than they ever will to a salesperson. This is an important fact of life.

5. *Small investment—big return.* Once your technical talent buys into the concept that when they influence with integrity, it is good for their customers, you are two-thirds of the way home. Because of the four points outlined above, all it takes is some building of existing skills and a road map on what to do, and they can

quickly start positively influencing services sales. While it might take years to get product sellers effectively selling services, your technical people can be productive in just months.

GIST: Getting your technical talent to help sell services should be a top priority.

How to Do It

Knowing how to positively leverage the trust built by your project managers, consultants, support account managers, and field engineers makes it easy to sell services (and products) that add value both to your customers and your organization.

Effectively done, you'll see qualitative changes in 30 days and quantitative results in three months. Here are the core steps to making it work:

Step One: Communicate That Professional Selling Is Not Evil
You've all probably heard this from your technical talent at one time or another: "If I'd have wanted to sell, I'd have gone into sales." I've heard this time and time again in my workshops on helping technical talent become more like consultants or helping them understand the attributes of trusted advisors. When this part of the workshop occurs, the body language of many of the technical people quickly changes—their arms cross, their bodies lean back in the chair, and their eyes roll.

When asked, "When you hear the word 'selling,' what thoughts come to mind?", the answers are predictable: "slick," "used-car salesman," "sleazy," and so on. This is truly a shame. Many of us let a few bad experiences early in life or stereotypes about salespeople (see the movie *Tin Men* for a great example of all that can be bad about selling) color our thoughts and attitudes toward what is one of the

Figure 9

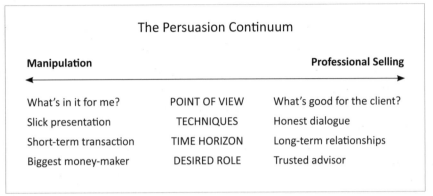

The Persuasion Continuum

Manipulation		Professional Selling
What's in it for me?	POINT OF VIEW	What's good for the client?
Slick presentation	TECHNIQUES	Honest dialogue
Short-term transaction	TIME HORIZON	Long-term relationships
Biggest money-maker	DESIRED ROLE	Trusted advisor

most challenging and important professions.

Figure 9, The Persuasion Continuum, sheds some insight on the differences between professional selling and manipulation.

Individuals whose persuasion philosophy is manipulation have the point of view of "what's in it for me." They don't care whether the sale is good for the customer, as long as they get the sale. To them, greed is good. Professional sellers, however, start with the mindset of "what's good for the client." They realize that creating client value will lead to value for them and their organization. Professional sellers understand the old maxim "you've got to give to get."

The manipulator relies on a slick presentation as the chosen technique for success. Formula selling skills (Attention-Interest-Desire-Response is a classic example) are used as an attempt to trigger buying behavior to coerce the prospect into buying whatever the seller wants to sell, whether the buyer needs it or not. Professional sellers, on the other hand, put a very high value on their personal integrity. Therefore, they prefer honest dialogue as their communication technique of choice. Providing straight talk about problems and fixes, what they know, and what they don't know, these folks tell it like it is because their personal credibility is on the line.

The time horizon of the manipulator is "right now." He or she is only interested in making today's numbers, this month's numbers, and the quarterly numbers. Nothing else matters. "Live for today" is the motto of the manipulator. Conversely, professional salespeople are in it for the long haul. Hopefully, they will be coming back to the client again and again. They know that a long-term relationship takes time and effort, but is worth the investment.

Finally, manipulators want to be showcased to their peers at the annual sales extravaganza in Hawaii as the biggest money makers—the top dogs. This is the ultimate recognition and the role they lust for. However, the professional seller's recognition comes from being seen as a trusted advisor. Nothing epitomizes success more than this achievement. When your clients call you over the weekend to ask your advice about an important personal issue that is totally non-related to business, you know you have reached this level. It is an awesome feeling.

> GIST: The truth is that your technical people are not acting professionally if they are not selling—that is, looking for customer problems or opportunities that your organization can positively address. Selling is servicing; it is as simple as that. Once they understand that selling, properly done, is good for their customers, most of your technical talent will be open to this important change in their role.

Step Two: Lay Out Baseline Expectations for Everyone in the Services Organization Who Touches the Customer
Figure 10 outlines the six levels of selling expectations for your technical talent, ranging from very passive to very aggressive. Following each expectation is an example communication from the technical person to the salesperson. I strongly suggest that you establish a minimum level of selling support for each of your services groups (project managers, account managers, consultants) and make this a central part of your expectations and their performance plan. It must be seen as a core part of the job, not a nice-to-do, but a must-do. For your people who really like selling, you may want to bump up their

Figure 10

The Six Business Development Expectations for Technical Talent

1. Focus on meeting services objectives and leave all business development tasks to sales:
   "Hi Carol. Just a quick update to let you know that the service call was successful."

2. When the customer mentions potential opportunities, communicate these opportunities to sales:
   "Hi Carol. I overheard Billie Owens, the operations manager at NewCo, complain to one of her people about how limited their valve repair process was. Thought you'd like to know."

3. Actively look and listen for customer opportunities, then pass them on to sales:
   "Hi Carol. In my weekly debriefing with Billie Owens, I asked her what other technical problems they were having. The attached document outlines what was shared related to their five biggest problems. Go get 'em!"

4. Actively look and listen for customer opportunities, qualify the customer need, then pass it on to sales:
   "Hi Carol. In my weekly debriefing with Billie Owens, I asked her what other technical problems were giving her fits. She outlined five issues that were her biggest challenges. I then proceeded to qualify those challenges and found that there were two issues she was serious about acting upon. Attached are my qualifying checklists for these two needs and a few notes. Good luck!"

5. Actively look, listen, and research opportunities, qualify the need, and work with sales to develop proposals:
   "Hi Carol. In my weekly debriefing with Billie Owens, I asked her what other problems were giving her fits. She outlined five issues that were her biggest challenges. I then proceeded to qualify those challenges and found that there were two issues she was serious about acting upon. Attached are my qualifying checklists for these two needs and a few notes. What does your schedule look like for Tuesday? Maybe we can set aside 45 minutes to plan our approach and create a proposal for these two new potential projects."

6. Actively look, listen, and research customer opportunities, qualify the need, develop the proposal, and present it to the customer:
   "Hi Carol. Just wanted to keep you in the loop. I'm pleased to say that Billie Owens, operations manager at NewCo, has agreed to two more projects! Attached you'll find the signed proposals and project plans. You'll note that the first one starts in two weeks. Let me know if you have any questions."

role a level or two.

As you review the expectations, determine where each of your technical groups are today and where they should be in a year or two.

As a reference point, Figure 11 shows the level of selling expectations for technical talent from my research. I've seen services executives ask more business development behaviors of their technical talent each year, but I was very surprised at the survey results. As you see in Figure 11, over 50% of expectations were very aggressive—at a level 5 or 6. This has some significant implications, as it is a fairly drastic change for those who were hired to "fix problems and make sure stuff works." More on this later.

Figure 11

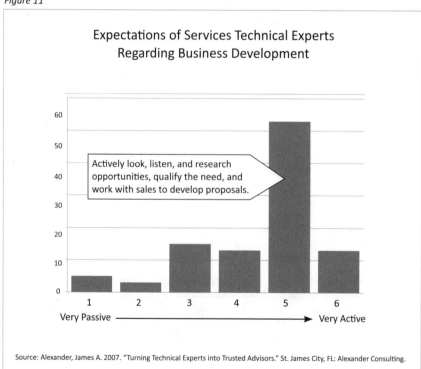

Expectations of Services Technical Experts Regarding Business Development

Actively look, listen, and research opportunities, qualify the need, and work with sales to develop proposals.

Very Passive ————————————→ Very Active

Source: Alexander, James A. 2007. "Turning Technical Experts into Trusted Advisors." St. James City, FL: Alexander Consulting.

Step Three: Provide Incentives That Motivate Your People

Recognition is always a strong motivator. I suggest starting small. For example, as some of your people attempt to be more aggressive in selling appropriately, acknowledge them both publically and privately. Feature them in your internal newsletters, buy them lunch— just show them you appreciate their efforts. Their peers will quickly try and get involved as well.

Step Four: Train Everyone on How to Build Relationships and Sell Services

Find some services industry-specific, high-involvement training that will give your people not only the appropriate skills for selling competence, but also improve their selling confidence. My experience shows that quality training will yield positive selling behaviors almost immediately.

Sure there are other considerations, but the above five steps are the main elements of getting your technical talent up and running on selling services.

Barriers to Plan For

Of course there are always a few challenges. Here are four that come up in most scenarios.

1. *It's not for everyone.* Yes, it is vital for your business today, but most of your technical people were probably hired with the sole focus of implementing, fixing, or problem solving. We owe it to them to provide them with the tools to make the change, but realize that a certain percentage (15% to 30%) won't do it; they just don't have the desire and/or the skills to do it. If you are serious about selling services, you'll need to find new roles for these people.

2. *Sales pushback.* Once they understand the program of technical people assuming some responsibility for selling, most top sellers in the sales force, your Ace Flanagans, welcome the services sell-

ing initiative, as they see it directly helps them to be more successful. Sellers in the middle will be a little leery but can be won over when they see the results. Usually, it is the lower-performing sellers that push back, expressing something along the lines of: "Those are my customers. I do the selling around here!" Most likely they feel threatened. Overcoming this mindset requires three things: (1) A good relationship with sales management and their support of having services people involved in selling, (2) not taking anything away from the sellers (they get their normal commission/bonus on everything your people sell), and (3) clearly defining who owns the customer when. For example, in many organizations, sales' main role is to find and sell big product deals, to act as "hunters." Once the initial deal is sold, it often makes sense to turn the account over to a "farmer" from services (often called a customer relationship manager or services account manager) to make sure the product is used correctly, issues are resolved quickly, and new opportunities are uncovered. For this system to work, however, the process needs to be clearly defined, and ownership must be determined at each step.

3. *Mixed metrics.* If you decide that you want some of your technical talent to be aggressive in selling, they will naturally have to invest more of their time in doing so. For example, you can't expect a consultant to invest two days a week in some sort of selling activity and remain 75% billable. So you will need to adjust expectations, objectives, and incentives to align with your new expectations.

4. *Going native.* My research on this topic (Alexander, 2007) clearly shows that services leadership's greatest fear is that their technical talent is perceived by the customer as crossing the line from being a technical expert there to help, to being a salesperson looking to sell them something. If this happens, the relationship will never be the same. The key is balance—driving home the concept that whatever the technical talent's position or title may be, their goal is to assume the role, when possible, of being seen as a trusted advisor. This takes vigilance, especially for some of

your people who really like to sell! The best way to keep this from happening in most situations is to keep incentives relatively small—big enough to get their attention, but small enough so that they don't go over to the "Dark Side."

GIST: Selling should be everyone's business, and your technical talent are a critical part of that mix. Define and implement a selling services strategy that is right for your organization, and you'll quickly reap the rewards.

Best Practices

1. *Get everyone who touches the customer on board.* So far we have talked about getting the salespeople, the sales managers, and technical talent on board and up to speed. Who's left? Everyone else who touches the customer, from phone contact personnel to managers to executives to the receptionist. With everything else going on, it is easy to forget or delay the communicating, training, and reinforcement needed for these important people.

   The approach outlined above applies to everyone in the organization. Understand the value of having everyone sell services (and products) professionally and what selling expectations are appropriate for them. Train them on what it takes to meet their selling expectations, and put incentives in place to motivate them to do the right thing.

2. *Put an emphasis on pre-sales support.* In many organizations that sell complex products into complex environments, technical specialists are an important part of the sales organization. They go by numerous titles, but for our purposes, let's call them SAs (solution architects). Immediately after an opportunity is discovered and qualified (at least to some degree) by the salesperson, the salesperson brings in the SA to "talk tech" with the custom-

er, understand the environment, and if the opportunity appears worth pursuing, takes the lead in creating a proposal. The role of the SA is to help sell, and they are compensated for it just like the salespeople. When it goes well, the SA and the salesperson become a strong team, with the salesperson finding opportunities and building business relationships, and the SA providing technical credibility and the knowledge to craft technically appropriate solutions.

However, when it comes to seriously selling services, often the same roadblocks discussed with the salespeople occur with pre-sales support. The SAs are often product specialists, and because of how their selling teammates (and themselves) are compensated, they have been trained to focus on the product and only consider the absolute minimum amount of services when crafting responses to customer needs. Hence, they need the same change in mindset, knowledge, and skills as the sellers. In most cases, it is good to train sellers and SAs simultaneously so that they can grapple with the change together. SAs that are competent and confident in selling services can be a huge help in bolstering the selling services capabilities of the product sales force.

3. *Establish dedicated services sellers.* When first making the move toward seriously selling services, a best practice is to bring some dedicated services selling horsepower on board—people who are already competent, confident, and credible in selling the type of services you need to sell. Doing this has many benefits:

- It demonstrates to your company your commitment to seriously selling services. Bringing in top services sellers is not cheap, and the signal made by your investment is strong.
- You will generate services revenue fairly quickly, helping to quell the natural fears that this initiative is not a good one.
- Once the dedicated services sellers start showing results, it will begin to remove the excuses of your product sellers that customers won't pay for services. Furthermore, this modeling will encourage some of the sales force to give it a try.

After a few years, when your general sales force has good services selling capability, you may go back to one sales force. However, initially hiring dedicated services sellers is a very good idea.

Conclusion

Getting the product sales force to effectively sell services is important to long-term success, but few organizations can sit back and wait while product sellers get up to speed. Everyone who touches the customer must have a role in selling services, and because of their existing customer relationships, technical people are the logical choice to initially focus on. Provide them with the knowledge, tools, skills, and incentives to be effective, and services sales will quickly follow.

CHAPTER 4

Transitioning from Free to Fee

Transitioning from free to fee has a nice ring to it, but how in the world do you do it without alienating your customers, de-motivating your sales force, and creating havoc in your organization? What is the correct strategy for your organization to start getting paid for the services you have been giving away? What types of services should you be selling?

This chapter is specifically for executives and services leaders in organizations that have given away services to customers in the past and now want to charge for them. You will learn that your task is more difficult compared to those who have little history providing services because you have trained your customers and your salespeople that services are free, and since they are free they can't be worth much! You'll discover the need to be prepared for the inevitable pushback to this change and what you must do to be ready to deal with it. You'll learn the five strategies for making this transition from free to fee and which strategy is most viable in most situations. You also will be provided with a customer-centric framework in which to view your current and potential services offerings, the three types of typical services you should be offering, and the vital importance of services contracts to most businesses.

The Five Strategies in Transitioning from Free to Fee

Strategy One: Don't Do It!

Just kidding. But when you realize all the potential grief you may get for leading this change, you may wish you hadn't started. More seriously, unless you are willing to rigorously do the steps outlined a little later on, you may want to wait.

Ponder Point: If it is worth doing, it takes effort—lots of effort.

If there is any question at all in moving from free to fee, I suggest that you do a quick readiness review that looks at your customer issues, competitive position, internal capabilities, and executive priorities. There is no sense attempting this transition unless there is enough rational reason and emotional impetus to justify this effort.

In leading workshops on building profitable services organizations over the last decade, one of the first exercises that I ask the executive participants to do is to complete a high-level, free-to-fee readiness review of their organization. It is a simple but powerful task that can be executed in less than 30 minutes. As the name implies, the readiness review helps determine how ready an organization is to make this transition. It helps executives determine the factors in place today that will either help or hinder the future goal of selling services. The focus is on the biggest, most important factors that will impact this transition.

Figure 12 provides an example of an executive's readiness review from one of my workshops. On the positive side, there were several helping factors in place that ideally could be leveraged to make the transition from free to fee successful. Having a large installed base meant lots of prospects for selling services. Customers who buy high-priced, complex products are more likely to spend money on services such as an insurance policy to improve uptime. Strong consultants and technical support personnel probably have a level of customer trust already established, hence if they recommend to customers that they buy services, the customer is likely to

Figure 12

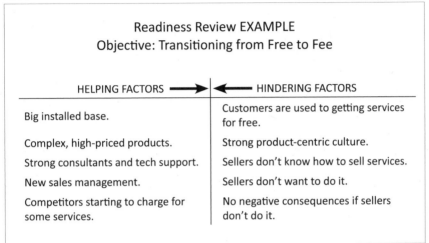

do so. Depending upon the new sales management's background and mindset, sales leadership may be open to selling the value of services. Finally, competitors selling services might serve as a lever to get senior management feeling the need to meet this potential challenge. Again, if the decision is made to move ahead with the free-to-fee strategy, the task is to leverage these helping factors to either eliminate or minimize the hindering factors.

On the hindering side, there were some significant factors to consider. The organization in this example had been giving services away forever, and customers expected it. The organization had a strong product culture, and as I've already emphasized, this is a big deal when trying to introduce change. Furthermore, sellers that don't want to sell services, don't know how to sell services, and have no negative consequences if they don't sell services are strong deterrents to getting customers to pay for services.

In this case, the executive learned that his task of transitioning from free to fee was a huge challenge, and after completing the readiness review, one that he doubted could be accomplished at all. After some consultation with me and his workshop peers, he decided that he needed to approach his boss with his assessment that the move from free to fee was not doable at this time. However, he was first going to get some fact-based information to back up his thinking and make a stronger business case. This 30-minute readiness review may have saved him months of toil and frustration.

How realistic is making the move from free to fee in your organization today?

> GIST: If the possibilities of success are small, wait for things to change—they always do.

Strategy Two: Flip the Switch

Ponder Point: If it seems easy, it probably won't work.

If you feel that free to fee can work in your organization, first consider flipping the switch. This strategy is based on picking a date in the future and letting everyone know that from that day forward, all services have fees attached to them. The positive side is that it is simple, it is fair from the standpoint of treating everyone the same, and if successful, it will quickly add a new revenue stream.

However, this is a difficult strategy to implement and manage. Within minutes of the announcement, the phones will start to ring as sellers call sales management, sales management calls your executives, and the execs call you (the services troublemaker, as you are beginning to be called), all saying the same thing: "Yes, we understand the need to charge for services, and as a rule I totally support it, but in this case it is not a good idea, because 'blah, blah, blah.'" The "blah, blah, blah" includes "we will lose a big pending sale because of our higher price," "the competition gives it away, and this will give them a wedge inside the company," or "the customer's policy is not to pay for any services," and similar-sounding reasons.

If you are initially able to fend off your people internally who are trying to twist your arm, the salespeople will collude and plot with customers, and soon the customers will start calling you, either pleading or threatening, or both. If you don't meet their demands, they will call senior management and senior management will cave. Therefore, the rule of everyone paying for all services very quickly becomes the exception as more and more customers are waived from having to pay. You spend all your time in defensive mode, making it hard for you to get the real work done.

GIST: Just don't do it. You will be hated, non-productive, and not much fun to be around.

Strategy Three: Grandfather Existing Customers

Ponder Point: You can fool some of the people some of the time, but not for long.

Under this strategy, all old customers are "grandfathered" and will continue to get services for free, however, all new customers are tagged to pay. The strength of this is that you don't rock the boat with the installed base, and new customers don't have a past history to compare what was and what is. Sold correctly, many new customers will pay, providing you with new revenue. The problem here, of course, is that customers talk, and new customers who find out about their second-class status will not be happy. They will see this approach as unfair and view themselves as victims. They will complain, and if they do it long enough and loud enough, they will probably get services for free as well. It will take a percentage of management time to deal with a problem that never goes away. Once again, you will be seen as "not a team player" and a "troublemaker."

GIST: Don't attempt this strategy either.

Strategy Four: Launch in New Markets

This strategy is a variation of Strategy Three, where all old customers are grandfathered in. However, if you are opening up new geographies or new market segments, this strategy can work, as customers in these spaces probably will be less likely to be in contact with your old customers. Plus you can make the case with some credibility that their situation is different and justifies that you charge for services. This approach is more feasible than Strategy Two or Strategy Three, but it is still a challenge to manage. Again, in most cases I do not recommend it, but it can work adequately in some situations.

Strategy Five: Productize the Old and Sell the New

Ponder Point: People will fight to keep what they have, so don't try to take away something they feel they deserve.

The problem with the strategies outlined above is that they trigger a powerful, negative psychological response—no one likes to have things taken away from them or not be treated the same as others. Think of your reaction to small personal takeaways, such as when your bank starts charging you for checks that used to be free, or your airline makes you pay for blankets.

Hence, this is the strategy I recommend almost always: Productize the old and sell the new. The beauty of this is that it takes nothing away from your customers or your sellers. In this scenario, all the services that have been given away continue to be given away, but in a cheaper, more manageable fashion. In addition, a new portfolio of value-adding services are developed, marketed, and sold. The other very positive psychology here is that it gives people an additional choice, and people like choices because it puts them more in control. The challenge is that this takes quite a bit of work in two areas:

1. *Productize the old.* Here the focus is to standardize the types of services that have been given away in the past to minimize the cost of these services and create a comparison that will make the new, fee-based, value-added services seem very desirable. For

example, when hoping to land a deal, in the past, sales may have given away assessments that had no definition of time or quality. In other words, sales would have had a pre-sales specialist do the assessment, or someone from the professional services group, or maybe they would even do the assessment themselves. It was based upon the availability of qualified people and the internal persuasion skills of the seller. Depending on the situation, it may have lasted anywhere from two days to five days at the customer's site. The quality of the assessment was totally dependent on the person performing it. In this situation, the goal of delivering an assessment may have been accomplished, but it was probably done in a haphazard, non-standardized manner—one that was not repeatable and one of questionable quality.

So the recommended shift is from an ill-defined, get-it-done-when-we-can, at-the-quality-level-of-whomever-we-can-get-to-do-it, on-average five-day assessment, to a one-day virtual assessment covering the 10 most important areas, delivered in a standardized, professional document, conducted by a qualified, trained professional. This new service and the other productized services (e.g., Quick Start installation for a software product, on-line core training for a customer administrator) are developed by services and marketing but are categorized as a cost of sales and owned by the sales function.

2. *Sell the new.* Building a high-value portfolio of services offerings that customers want and will pay for and one you will make good money on takes considerable effort. Plus, correctly defining, packaging, and pricing these services may take skills not currently available in your organization.

GIST: This is a lot of work and will take a few months of effort to accomplish. However, this approach is far superior to the other strategies, as it gives more to the customer and to sales without taking anything away.

Chapter 5 will outline the services portfolio framework and the 10-step approach for what it takes to do it right.

The Three Types of Services Offerings

To keep things simple, I've categorizing services into three groupings: start-up services, up-time services, and professional services.

Start-Up Services

The objective of start-up services is simple: Get the product (the "box") up and running right the first time (Figure 13). Examples vary across the board by industry and company, from installing imaging equipment in a hospital to implementing security software for a bank to commissioning a new production facility for an aircraft manufacturer. Whoever performs them, customers must have these services to derive the promised value from their newly purchased products. In some cases, customers can easily perform the services themselves, but the more important and complex the scenario, the more likely it is that they will be amenable to outside help. An important point to note is that if it is your hardware or software, your organization is their preferred choice, as they see you as the expert.

Figure 13

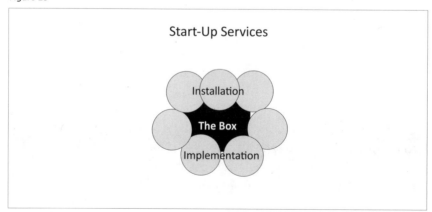

You have several choices. You can offer to do the complete start-up from beginning to end, train the customer how to do it, or work with the customer to transfer knowledge and make sure it gets done right. Many organizations will offer their customers all three choices. Someone has to do start-up services, so it might as well be you.

Uptime Services

Once the product is up and running, customers want to keep it that way. The more important your products are to the customer and the more complex the environment in which they operate, the more desirable customers view offerings that can minimize downtime and, thus, positively impact productivity. Typical uptime services might include preventive maintenance, break-fix services, technical support, customer training on the product, or remote monitoring and diagnosing (Figure 14).

Figure 14

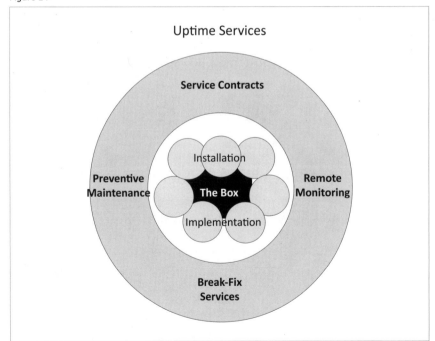

Uptime services can be delivered on-site, over the phone, by e-mail, or through self-service via the Internet. These services can be priced by incidence or by the hour (for example, $150 per hour plus parts for an on-site visit), but savvy services providers always recommend packaging their uptime services in the form of services contracts, traditionally in three levels: basic (Bronze), intermediate (Silver), and comprehensive (Gold). In most cases, the more the customer is willing to spend, the more access he or she has to information and expertise, and the greater the supplier's commitment to resolve issues faster. Services contracts define the roles, responsibilities, and performance metrics that your organization will take to quickly resolve product issues when they occur (or better yet, prevent the problems from occurring in the first place).

Customers like services contracts. As Figure 15 shows, there are three important reasons. First, services contracts eliminate or minimize downtime, thus directly impacting productivity. For example,

Figure 15

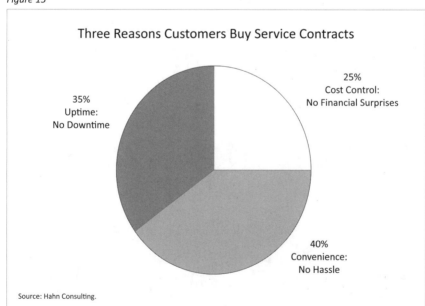

Source: Hahn Consulting.

if your product is part of a production line that costs the customer thousands of dollars an hour when it is down, they will gladly pay handsomely for a services contract that reduces that risk, as the return on investment makes very good business sense.

Second, customers don't like surprises. Most prefer to add a line item in the budget for a pre-determined cost of service rather than run the risk of big, unexpected product repair costs that require special requests and executive approvals that might question the competence of the person doing the requisition. Once this line item is in the budget, it tends to stay there year after year.

And third, services contracts minimize customer hassle. If a product failure brings an assembly line down at 2:00 a.m., the frantic call from the factory floor supervisor or the data center manager goes to the supplier services organization, and not to the person who signed the services contract. No muss, no fuss, the supplier assumes the burden of uptime. These are powerful benefits to most customers—no wonder it is not uncommon for many services organizations to have over 90% of their customers covered by services contracts.

Services contracts are the lifeblood of a services business. They allow services management to accurately predict future profitable income, which then allows them to build manpower plans and budgets. Hence, focusing on building the highest value (that which customers want, will pay for, and are profitable to you), targeting the content of services contracts should be a cornerstone of your customer research, as will be described shortly. Finding out what your customers value should be used as direct inputs into the types of contracts you offer.

There are even more benefits when your services organization sells lots of contracts. Customers with services contracts are more likely to buy your products in the future (and, of course, the services contracts that go with them). This is a beautiful thing.

But there is even more. Since people from your organization—services account managers, field engineers, professional services consultants—are routinely interacting with the customer, they are developing personal relationships along the way. By being responsive and reliable in handling issues that do occur, trust is built. The ongoing contact alerts your people to potential problems that can be averted and uncovers new opportunities that can lead to more business. This is one of the most powerful ways to expand customer sales, improve efficiencies, and lock out the competition.

My recommendation? Sell services contracts!

Professional Services

Sometimes called value-added services, professional services go "beyond the box," impacting customer processes or systems that have the potential to add much more value to the business than uptime services. Professional services can be sold and implemented before the product is sold, after the product is sold, or while the product is being started up. Professional services are created from the specialized expertise resident in your people.

Figure 16

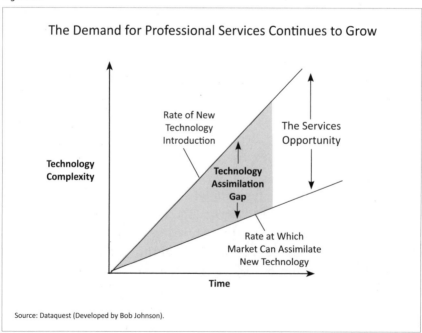

The Demand for Professional Services Continues to Grow

Source: Dataquest (Developed by Bob Johnson).

As Figure 16 shows, the demand for professional services is strong and continuing to grow. The reason is that as new technologies are introduced, there is an assimilation gap—a time lag in which organizations learn how to use the new technology productively. Proper use of specialized expertise in the form of professional services can help customers close that gap so that they receive a faster return on their technology investments.

More and more executives at product companies are looking at the professional services potential. Figure 17 shows that over 80% of executives in one of my studies said that professional services was either an important topic of discussion or a business priority.

Figure 18 shows examples of the most common professional services offerings.

Figure 17

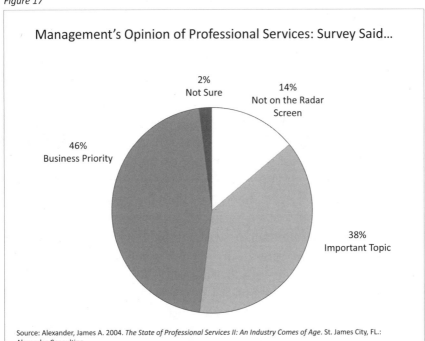

Management's Opinion of Professional Services: Survey Said...

2% Not Sure

14% Not on the Radar Screen

46% Business Priority

38% Important Topic

Source: Alexander, James A. 2004. *The State of Professional Services II: An Industry Comes of Age*. St. James City, FL.: Alexander Consulting.

Figure 18

Assessments

If your organization is trying to sell complex solutions, assessments are a must. How can you recommend answers to complicated issues without having a solid understanding of the situation? Well-done assessments help both you and your customer to better understand the issues and options and, hence, develop the most appropriate responses.

If you sell and deliver an assessment early in the customer buying process, two more benefits arise. First, you have the opportunity to start building relationships at all levels of the customer organization. Second, you have the opportunity to shape buying parameters for the solution (RFPs, for example) and lock out the competition. If for whatever reason you choose to begin offering just one professional service, this is it.

The Five Approaches to Selling Assessments

As a rule, top-performing sellers always recommend/require/ sell an assessment as a key event early in their selling cycle. Not only does a well-done, up-front assessment shape the requirements of the larger engagement, but it minimizes risk, demonstrates credibility, and builds executive relationships.
 Here are your pricing/positioning choices:
* *Price at full value plus expenses.* Try to maximize what you can get for the assessment and not worry a lot about future business. If the assessment is worth $50,000, charge $50,000.
* *Price at a discount plus expenses.* In this approach you may feel that the assessment is worth $50,000, but you might price it at $20,000. You do this to improve the probability of making this sale as well as getting the follow-up business. To justify the discount, you might position your prospect as an important account strategic to your organization. Hence, you are willing to sacrifice early revenue in the hope of building a long-term relationship.
* *Price at full value or at a discount plus expenses, but agree to credit the prospect the full amount of the assessment if they purchase the next phase from you.* Assuming the prospect liked your work, this puts you in good stead to win the next phase.
* *Price only at expenses.* Again you might position the prospect as a strategic account, thus you are willing to invest in the prospect. Of course, this will take some internal discussion and negotiation since a department will have to absorb this cost of sale.
* *Price only at expenses with a fee for the report.* This is also a strategic investment in the account. Orally share your findings and recommendations with executives, but don't hand over the report unless the prospect pays the predetermined value.*

Audits

While assessments are done up-front to help determine the most appropriate recommendations, audits are performed after a project is completed or a solution is up and running. Audits are most often used to determine if the results achieved are the results that were anticipated (or in some cases required). Furthermore, audits based on industry benchmarks and best practices can provide a "quality report" on whoever did the implementation. Audits can be a good way to try to oust a competitor and gain a foothold into new clients.

Project Management

If your organization sells complex engagements, someone has to manage them. Sometimes your customer does not have qualified people to assume this role, so the success of the project is at risk unless you or another outside organization manages it for them.

In other instances the customer has qualified people in-house, but may find it attractive to keep their people focused on other projects if alternative choices for project management are available. For most mature services businesses, project management is the most, or one of the most, profitable offerings. Odds are that you have one or more people who have these capabilities right now, so this is a service that could be offered immediately.

Advanced Training

In all the customer research that my firm has helped clients to implement over the years, advanced training is always one of the offerings most wanted by the customer. Customers quickly see the need for more training, they like training, their people want training, and often it is already budgeted. Offer it in a public setting in various geographies, customize it to specific customers, make it available face-to-face, over the phone, via Webinars, and as computer-based training.

In most professional services organizations, training should contribute 15% or more to the total revenue. Furthermore, ramping up advanced training programs usually can be done quickly, and thus fund services that take longer to develop.

Process Improvement

If, for example, you sell copiers and printers, your products might well be important components in your customers' data flow network. Odds are you have some internal expertise on how to best manage the flow of information in many different settings, and thus might be able to help package your know-how to improve your customers' processes. Furthermore, customers will expect and accept your process improvement services readily, as they associate your services expertise with your product expertise, with which they are already familiar.

Hence, process improvement is a natural service for most organizations to develop and sell, whether your products are a part of information flow, data management, supply chain, or security networks. There are many pure services companies, such as consulting firms, that offer process improvement services, but if you are an OEM selling products within these processes, you will be seen as the expert.

Certifications

Sometimes you may choose to have services performed by partners (VARs, distributors, dealers, manufacturing reps, independent services organizations). However, from the customers' viewpoints, if they own your products, you are responsible for the quality of the service no matter who provides it. This is not always fair, but it is true nonetheless. Therefore, it is critical that you choose trustworthy, competent partners and make sure that they know what they are doing. You should be providing this knowledge and these skills anyway, so why not get paid for it? Make it a requirement that anyone who offers your services be certified by your organization. This is a great quality-control mechanism and also a good revenue stream

For customers who prefer to self-service, this is another service you can offer them, and some will value it. Of course, to become certified, services personnel from your partners will need to successfully attend your training and demonstrate their ability to do the services activities that you have determined are important and required. An entire training curriculum might be called for with the potential for various levels of certification based upon proven competence.

There will be more on the challenges of dealing with partners in Chapter 6.

Other Potential Professional Services

Depending on the type of business you are in, the needs of your customers, and your capabilities, there are many other professional services possibilities to consider now and in the future, such as asset management, systems integration, system optimization, database services, or load testing. If you have broad knowledge across technologies, your customers may be open to purchasing technology consulting from you. In addition, if you have established high levels of credibility, some organizations may be receptive to you providing management consulting, such as strategy formulation and change management.

Furthermore, if you have the capabilities and the desire, certain customers will be interested in purchasing managed services from you, giving you responsibility for important tasks or possibly outsourcing certain parts of the business to you.

There you have a high-level view of the most common types of services. Use this as a guide as you move through the steps to building a robust portfolio of offerings in Chapter 5.

Best Practices in Transitioning from Free to Fee

1. *Conduct a readiness review.* Spend some time up-front to establish/confirm that transitioning from free to fee is worth the effort. If you don't have enough information to convince yourself and other executives, expand your review until you get the facts you need.

2. *Radically change the selling compensation plan.* This is really quite simple. Change rewards from maximizing sales volume to maximizing profitability of the total sale, or at least to meet a minimum profitability benchmark. If enforced, those same sellers

who wouldn't think twice about throwing in a year's worth of support or 100 hours of consulting to clench a deal, now (with calculator in hand) will approach every sale from a different perspective. If they decide to give away or discount services, they do so at their own peril, as they endanger taking their spouse to the President's Council trip in Barcelona or jeopardize maxing out their total compensation.

Of course, two things must happen, and they are not easy to do. First, get the executive team to agree on changing the sales incentive focus from driving volume alone to driving profitable revenue. It requires a fact-loaded, everybody-wins business case to sell this shift...(plus patience). It also raises the important discussion of blended margins and the overall profitability of solutions sales. Once senior management sees the overall financial impact, they will become true believers of the cause. Second, make sure that the sales force is capable of selling services appropriately—could they do it if you put a gun to their head? Follow the approach outlined in Chapter 2.

3. *Partner with the vice president of sales to determine acceptable giveaways.* Yes, you should charge for services, but there will always be exceptions. It is better to know the rules up-front, and even better if the vice president of sales is the one in charge of managing them.

4. *Make it a mandatory job requirement that your sellers present the benefits of services at the time of the product sale and customers have to say no not to buy them.* A common, but powerful example is when buying products online, the customer must accept or decline a services contract before completing the product buying transaction. This simple act will almost magically increase your attach rate 10% or more.

5. *Trust but verify.* Use follow-up customer satisfaction phone calls to confirm that sales did, in fact, position services up-front as described, and report this data throughout the organization. Letting go of a seller who does not follow this policy sends a very strong message throughout the organization.

Conclusion

Transitioning from free to fee is a major change and may not be for everyone. It is worth the time to conduct a readiness review to determine the probability of success, the factors needing the most attention, and an estimate of the effort needed to make it work.

For the majority of organizations making this transition, only one strategy is effective. This strategy consists of two components: First, streamlining and standardizing a core set of services that you will continue to provide at no cost, and second, creating a robust, high-value portfolio of new offerings to give your customers choices. If this strategy is wholeheartedly adopted, giving away services will become the exception, not the rule.

Creating High-Value Services:
Ten Steps to Profitable Growth

What services can you offer that customers want to buy? What is the best way to prioritize services development by importance? What is the most effective process to building services right the first time? How about pricing, and packaging, and promotion?

As noted in the previous chapter, building a portfolio of services offerings that customers want and will pay for is a required component of transitioning from free to fee. However, a robust, high-value services portfolio is more than that. It is the foundation of services business success.

In this chapter you will learn a 10-step model for launching new services and find out how to better manage your services portfolio. You'll discover how to use the voice of the customer as a powerful cornerstone in creating high-value services offerings that customers want to buy.

Services Marketing Critical Issues

Figure 19 shows that launching new services and managing the portfolio of offerings makes up over one-third of the critical services marketing issues identified by services executives. If we add in pricing, which is an important part of the services portfolio development process, then we see that well over 50% of marketing issues revolve around the creation of a robust services portfolio. Hence the need to get it right the first time.

Launching new services or refining your existing portfolio of offerings does not have to be expensive or take a lot of time. Figure 20 displays the 10 steps to launching new services. (In almost all situations, the 10 steps are the way to go. However, on rare occasions a speedier approch is required. See the sidebar on page 102 , to deter-

Figure 19

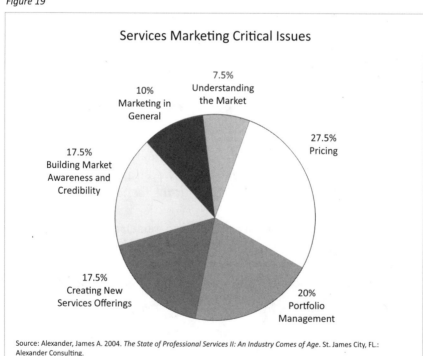

Source: Alexander, James A. 2004. *The State of Professional Services II: An Industry Comes of Age*. St. James City, FL.: Alexander Consulting.

Figure 20

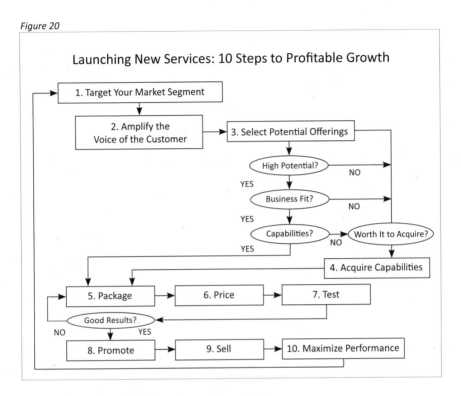

mine when fast-tracking is appropriate.)

GIST: Follow these steps, and you'll be successful...don't, and you won't.

Step One: Target Your Market Segment

Being effective in business is all about focus, and the same holds true when building services offerings. My philosophy is to start small and act quickly to get started in areas where you have the highest probability of success. This builds credibility both inside and outside your services business, plus you can use these early profits to fund new services and expand your services portfolio.

Here are the core market segmentation questions that need to be answered before starting the research:

1. *What type of customers should we target: prospective, existing, or past?* In building services offerings, my strong bias is to target existing customers. In almost all cases, the best prospects for new services are your best existing customers, be they purchasers of services or products or both. Mining the installed base is the most effective and most efficient place to start. Appropriately approached, your best existing customers gladly will take the time to share with you the key elements you need to know to develop and launch high-impact, differentiated services that are easy to sell.

2. *What market space should we target: geography, industry, function, or targeted accounts?* Start with the spaces in which you have good reason to have the biggest potential for services (e.g., some key accounts have expressly asked for new services, you've just launched new products targeted at an industry or function, strategically your company is trying to expand into a new geography). Again, take advantage of what you know to be important.

3. *What level of people should we target within the customers we have chosen: executives, managers, end users?* If you are mainly targeting uptime services, you'll need to emphasize talking to the managers who have that buying/operating responsibility, and possibly augment your interviews with a few end users. However, if you are looking to expand into professional services, you'll want to make sure that you get adequate customer executive input along with customer managers. The more important an offering is to a customer, the higher up the buying decision goes, so customer executives need to be part of the process. Note that if you are new to providing advanced services, the people inside your company may not know who the executives are.

4. *What size customers are we focusing on: enterprise, mid-market, or the small guys?* This is important, as the issues may be different based upon the size of the organizations you are looking at. Even if the basic issues are the same among your different sizes of cus-

tomers, the weighting of importance might vary. Base this decision on your overall strategy.

Step Two: Amplify the Voice of the Customer

Step One defines your population—the specific market segments that you'd like to explore building and offering services to. Step Two helps define your research sample and how to get the right information from these customers to make good business decisions about the services you will provide.

First, though, let's talk about what *not* to do.

The Big Mistake in Building a Portfolio of Services

I'm disappointed to say that the most common approach to building services offerings is not a best practice, but a worst practice. This approach is what I call "by guess and by golly." In this scenario, when I recommend conducting customer research to best determine which services to offer and what they should look like, my clients often tell me, "We already know what our customers want, and we don't have the time or budget to waste on research." This "we know best" approach is cheap and fast, but sadly predictable: Customer needs are only partially addressed, chances for differentiation are botched, internal resources are misdirected, and new volumes of higher-profit services revenue are left for someone else to capture. No wonder one-half of new services offerings are considered failures!

To strengthen the point, here is a real-life example: I was asked by a vice president of professional services from a Fortune 100 product company to come in and spend a day with her managers from around the globe. The newly formed organization had a year's experience, and she wanted to build plans to take her group to the next level of performance. In the discussion it became obvious that their services sales performance was way below expectation. When I asked to see the research data that they used to develop their services, the room became pin-drop quiet. Finally, the sheepish response was that there was no customer data. A year earlier this same group gathered in this same conference room around flip charts for two days and came up with services they *thought* customers wanted! Sadly, I see this same scenario played over and over again. In this case, they had wasted an entire year of opportunity, as well as frustrating their people and their customers.

Ponder Point: If you think you know what your customers want, need, and will pay for, you are probably wrong.

VOC: Building a Services Portfolio the Right Way

Voice of the customer (VOC) is a proven research method that gathers deep and rich information from in-depth personal interviews with key people from key accounts. Because it focuses on critical issues and involves important players, VOC has the power to create new, high-level relationships and motivate customers to act.

Ideal for when an organization wants to make a significant change with regard to its key customers' interest in potential new services, VOC tracks current usage of existing services and collects research about future services that could be developed to align with customers' future goals and direction. VOC also uncovers what their experience has been with other companies from whom they buy services. Oftentimes, interviewing a dozen customer companies per market segment is all that you'll need. The outcomes will be a very good understanding of the issues, needs, wants, and expectations of your key accounts, their experience with the services you asked about, their thoughts about you and your best competitors, and of course, the information and the rationale you need to help you sort through possible offerings.

GIST: VOC is a powerful process that works, it can be completed in 90 days, and it doesn't have to take a lot of money to do it. If you are serious about services, use VOC.

Step Three: Select Potential Offerings

If you've done the VOC research properly, you'll have identified several possible services offerings—ones your customers need, want, and seem willing to pay for. But all services offerings are not equal in importance. A few more questions need to be answered:

1. *Which offerings are high-potential?* Does it look like there is a large enough stream of profitable revenue to make it worth your while to develop and launch a particular service? Use the customer findings and the educated guess of your services portfolio team to rank them by potential revenue and profit over time (say, three years).

2. *Is it really a good business fit?* Would development of these services offerings align and support your key technologies and strategic direction? Some offerings may have very good potential and match up quite well with the direction of your services organization and your company, and others don't. Again, score or rank services according to business fit.

3. *Do you have the capabilities in place today (people, processes, technology) to build and deliver them?* This is an important issue, as it directly relates to how quickly services can be launched and the investment required. Sometimes all you need to do is re-assign a few personnel, and you are ready to go. Other services might require a significant investment. My feeling is not to avoid any services that have high potential and are a good business fit, just give the low-hanging fruit the priority.

4. If you don't have the capabilities today, you'll need to ask one more question: *Is it worth it to acquire new capabilities?* Part of the answer is straightforward and is arrived at by asking: Does the probable ROI over time make sense? The second part requires more strategic consideration: How important is this new offering to your future? Will adding this service help protect our product position in the marketplace? What are the competitive actions of not taking action? Answering this question might require getting input from other departments as well as senior management.

Step Four: Acquire Capabilities

Depending on the potential offering, this could be as simple as buying some new software or adding new headcount, or as involved as forging a new partnership or buying another company.

Almost all of the time, the most important capabilities you'll need to obtain are the expertise of experienced people. Once you've identified the results you want and the mandatory knowledge, skills, and experience needed, you face another choice, which is build, borrow, or buy. Each choice of course has plusses and minuses.

Here is a simple example: Let's say that you've decided that providing fee-based online customer training has excellent potential, and you have committed to designing and launching a number of courses. You envision this becoming a big revenue contributor over time and feel it will build more interest in your products and help strengthen the loyalty of your customers.

You realize that you'll need to acquire capabilities you don't have today. First you'll need the skills for effectively designing and delivering online courses for adults, and second you'll need to acquire the technology to deliver the training and measure performance. Here are your choices:

- *Build.* Post the jobs internally, find a couple of people with the desire and, hopefully, the capacity to learn, and send them off to school. During that time, research and buy the requisite technology. Maybe in six months you will be able to pilot your first program, learning as you go.

- *Borrow.* Interview several companies that do this for a living and select one to partner with. Have them bring in their learning professionals to interview your subject-matter experts, and within 60 days three programs are built and running on their system. Based upon that success, you contract with them to complete a robust portfolio.

- *Buy.* Have your business development people (or hire a consultant to do it for you) uncover a few online learning companies that are available for purchase and pursue them. Depending on your need and the availability of good acquisition targets, an alternative might be to try to find a highly qualified person or two and hire them away from another company.

Another option is following a hybrid strategy. For example, partner with an organization to get things going quickly while building your own capabilities and easing out the partner over time.

GIST: There are trade-offs with all three options: time to market, probable quality level, start-up and ongoing costs, management requirements, and business risk. Spend the time to think these through.

More on the build-borrow-buy decision-making process and tools will be covered in Chapter 6.

Step Five: Package

In the invisible world of services, customers consider everything they see, hear, and feel related to and surrounding your service as part of the package: your brochures, your Web site, your contracts, your written and verbal communications, your facilities, the events you sponsor, your people they come in contact with—even how they dress, how they talk, and the type and condition of the vehicles they drive. Your market message is embodied via your packaging and helps to emotionally connect (or not connect) your services and your organization with your customers.

All of these packaging components impact customer perception of your services and your services organization and help shape their expectations. The lesson for services management is that everything that surrounds your services is packaging, and it all matters. Services management should take the time to think through the image and brand they want their services business and individual services line to convey, and work to get a consistent look and feel in everything and everyone that touches the customer in every way. For example, if you are trying to convey the message that your services are world class (pricey, but worth it), then everything that is heard, seen, and felt by your customers should be indicators of world class—from the high-quality paper your sales collaterals are printed on to the leather chairs in your lobby to name-recognized speakers at your events. If you are trying to convey a no-nonsense, "we get 'er done" brand, your packaging should be more modest, with laminated furniture in your foyer, off-the-rack sport coats on your sellers, and Holiday Inns as the location for your meetings, all signifying that your emphasis is on the work, not the "fluff."

> GIST: In the rush and commotion to get new services offerings launched or refined, don't forget the importance of packaging and its long-term impact on your services business.

Step Six: Price

Ponder Point: Assuming that your service offering is a good match for your clients' needs, nothing has more impact on your overall profitability than your pricing. Nothing.

In this section on pricing you'll learn how customers' evaluations of services differ from their evaluations of products, the different methods available for pricing services, my recommended approach to pricing, and why I have a preference for fixed-fee pricing.

How Customers Evaluate Price
There are three key differences between customers' evaluations of pricing services versus products (Zeithaml and Bitner, 2000).

1. *Limited reference points.* In most situations, customers can fairly easily compare products by features and functions. For example, a purchasing agent interested in buying laptops for his field services organization could find Brand X with the characteristics he wants, and manually or with the use of shopping bots check the Web for pricing for that brand and model. He could also comparison-shop several other laptops of different makes, comparing apples to apples. However, that same purchasing agent interested in finding prices on services contracts on those same laptops has a much more challenging task. There is no such thing as a "standard" services contract; every services organization defines them differently. Plus, while it is common to find product pricing complete with descriptions on the Web, or with a minimum amount of effort obtain a price sheet from a salesperson, it is almost impossible to find that same information about services. In fact, on many product company Web sites, it is a major task to learn in any detail about services at all! So, when comparing services pricing, buyers often have inadequate data or misleading information and must beware of comparing apples to oranges.

2. *Price signals quality.* With limited reference points to compare, buyers often will see price as a key indicator of quality in services. So if all things appear relatively equal to the buyer, a higher price triggers the perception of higher quality. This is a powerful tenet. A corollary of this principle is that the market leader, again as perceived by the buyer, is both allowed and expected to take a 20% to 25% price premium. Therefore, if your company and/or product brand is very strong and is premium-priced, you must price your services at a premium as well. This is quite an advantage.

3. *There is more to price than just money.* The amount of dollars, euros, or yen being asked is, of course, important, but this is not the only component of price that buyers consider. Although rarely made public by the buyer, the perceived hassle associated with the purchase is another very important element of price. Buyers may feel that the monetary price is fair, but choose a competitor or not

purchase the service at all if they feel it creates an unwarranted demand on their time or if it is painful to buy your offering.

Pricing Methods

Thirty years ago or so, when services departments inside of product companies were starting to understand services and services contracts and their value both to customers and their businesses, they came across a brilliant way to price services. It was brilliant because it was extremely simple, easy to understand, and profitable. It was based on figuring out how much profit they wanted to make on their services and services contracts, then determining what the ratio was between the amount of money they wanted and what their equipment sold for. This "percentage of list" pricing worked as such: If a mainframe computer cost the customer $1 million, the services contract was, say, 15% of that price, or $150,000 per year. It was as simple as that. It was easy for salespeople to understand and easy for the customer to accept.

However, there are some negatives with this pricing method. First, because customers were "trained" by services organizations to view this pricing method as the norm, they started thinking of services as commodities. They then used this against suppliers to negotiate lower prices, even though, as I stated before, apples often were being compared with oranges. This could work against you. For example, your services contract might include A plus B plus C plus D, but your competitor does not include D. Hence, assuming that D added value, the customer might go with your competitor on price, assuming that what you both offered was the same. Not good.

Furthermore, as customers became accustomed to this method of pricing, they accepted it as the standard. Let's go back to the mainframe example. Due to competitive pressures, in a few years the equivalent to the $1 million mainframe was being sold for $800,000. However, customers still expected to pay 15% (or less) for services, even though the calculations used to compute this percentage had changed. Customers now expected to pay $120,000 for services, not the $150,000 they used to pay when the mainframe cost more. Obviously, this has the potential to negatively impact profitability. Finally, there was one more problem inherent from the get-go: Percentage of list pricing was totally supplier-centric and had no relationship to customer value.

GIST: Percentage of list is a worst practice in pricing services. Don't do it.

Here is the pricing strategy I recommend, using three other accepted pricing methods. Use all three of them when possible, in the order outlined below:

1. *Value-based.* The best definition of value that I know is that "value is what the customer will pay for." Here is where you need to start. Each customer is different, but if you've done your VOC research well, you quickly learn the common attributes your customers want.

   Realistically, how much value can your services deliver? Can you make a persuasive case that by purchasing services contracts, you can increase production line uptime from 94% to 97%, thus potentially saving your customer $5 million per year? If so, you have a strong value proposition. Can you demonstrate that by purchasing your security assessment and implementing its recommendations, you can decrease the chance of a network security breech by 70%? How much is that worth to the customer in stress relief alone?

   Starting from the standpoint of the customer, value keeps your customers interested, your marketers honest, and forces your salespeople to hone their listening and questioning skills to understand value from each and every customer's perspective.

Ponder Point: On average, most customers are willing to spend about 10% of the value they think they will receive from an offering, either product or service.

2. *Competitor comparison.* Competitor comparison is your reality check. Yes, you may be able to quantify and convince a customer of a probable increase in sales or a decrease in operating expense, however, if it is an important decision, often there will be competition. Remember that there is a 20% to 25% elasticity as I pointed out before, but even if the customer knows you have a better offering, going beyond that percentage puts you in a vulnerable competitive position. Your buyer may have to justify her decision to others internally, and the 25% premium is about the most that people buy into. Hence, the solid market intelligence uncovered in the VOC helps you determine what realistic pricing boundaries for pricing your services are.

3. *Gross margin hurdle.* Only now is it time to compare how your projected profitability compares with your organization's minimum acceptable gross margin level. Of course, however, this approach is only valuable if you really understand all of your costs and have them quantified appropriately; many organizations don't.

Approaches to Pricing Services

Although most services organizations will use all three pricing approaches from time to time, Figure 21 shows the most preferred approach to pricing services, taken from a survey of 157 services organizations (Alexander, 2004).

You will see that currently 50% of the study respondents stated that time-and-materials was their most common pricing method, 45% said fixed pricing, and 5% said pay-for-performance pricing.

This is a ratio that needs to change. Asking your customers to pay time-and-materials (pay by the pound) is a seller-centric pricing strategy designed to eliminate your risk and guarantee that you get the profit margin you desire. It presents no incentive to be more efficient; in fact, the temptation is to be inefficient, tacking on hours and days to maximize project revenue, or using the project to train your "green beans" on the client's nickel.

Think about this from the prospect's side of things: Have you ever been in a cab, and what you expected to be a $20 trip turns out

Figure 21

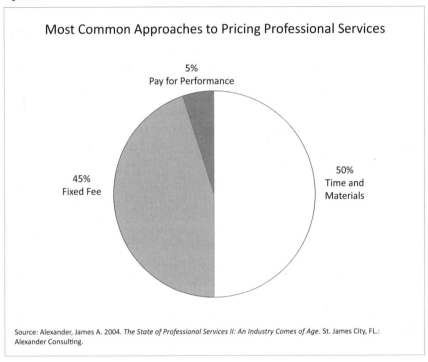

Most Common Approaches to Pricing Professional Services

5%
Pay for Performance

45%
Fixed Fee

50%
Time and
Materials

Source: Alexander, James A. 2004. *The State of Professional Services II: An Industry Comes of Age.* St. James City, FL.: Alexander Consulting.

to be a $50 fare? What did you think of the cabbie? Would you willingly travel with him or her again? People are conscious, and often a little nervous, when a meter is running. If you doubt me, just ask your customers!

Yes, asking customers to buy by fixed price (pay for the promise) makes your job a little more challenging, as you must couple strong discovery with solid experience to accurately estimate your costs. That is why assessments are so valuable. And yes, you are taking on some risk if you get it wrong. But well-thought-out, value-based fixed pricing can deliver the double-dip of higher margins and stronger client relationships by directing the conversation away from billing rates to bang-for-the-buck. Sell the way your customers want to buy, and make fixed pricing your primary pricing strategy.

If for whatever reason you feel you must charge by time-and-materials (a few customers prefer this approach), then segment pricing by the talent levels of your professional task (higher capability, higher rate) and charge extra when "above and beyond" efforts are required.

Along with a value-based, fixed-fee price, consider providing an option in which you assume some risk and link the accomplishment of objectives to compensation (along with an upside for surpassing goals). This demonstrates confidence, separates you from the competition, and reinvents the buying-purchasing paradigm.

Step Seven: Test

As with most all things that are important, it pays to pilot. Even following the thoughtful, rigorous approach outlined above, a surprise or two might pop up. So test your new services offerings to maximize the probability of launching them right the first time.

Where to test? Go with the folks who are trying to drag you into the future—the innovative customers who want you to succeed, the customers who love you even when you screw up. Sound familiar? It sounds a lot like the customers that you (hopefully) chose to contribute to the VOC research. Once you've gone through the first six steps above, schedule appointments with the people you interviewed during your customer research, and tell them what you learned and what you are doing about it. Since the services you are building are highly likely to be ones they want, this is a great place to start. My experience shows that at least 15% of your VOC customers will agree to immediately participate in a pilot, and a majority of the remainder will buy some of your new services within a year.

GIST: Not only does testing work out any bugs, it does something even more important—it provides you with reference accounts.

Step Eight: Promote

The goal of promoting is to get "suspects," or key individuals within your defined market, to contact your organization. First, they must become aware of your organization and your services offerings, and then be interested enough to proactively reach out to you; this is not an easy task. Once again, it is best to start from the perspective of a potential buyer and discover how buyers determine the solutions they will consider.

Figure 22 shows how technology executives (CIOs in this case)

Figure 22

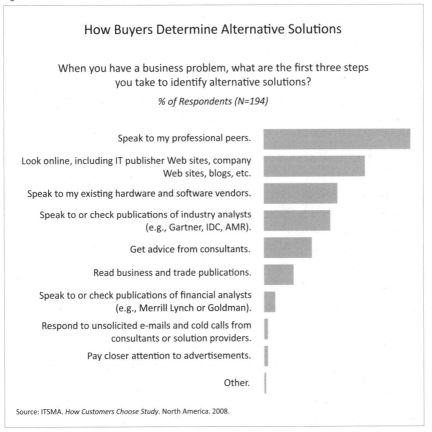

Source: ITSMA. *How Customers Choose Study.* North America. 2008.

decide which possible solutions to explore. All deserve some consideration, but let's focus on the top three. When executives face important complex buying decisions, their number one resource in determining how they will address it is contact with their peers—a quick phone call to an association member asking who she used for X and what she thought of them, or a lunch conversation at a company retreat asking a counterpart in a different geography who they use for Y and if they would recommend them. They tap into the knowledge and experience of peers either inside or outside their organization.

That means that a prime directive of every services marketer should be to create a large stable of respected executives who love your offerings and are very willing to talk about it. One of the most effective ways to package that message is through case studies in print, on the Web, or even better, coming out of your customer's mouth.

Ponder Point: Nothing works better in tangibilizing the intangible than having a customer executive brag about how your offerings made him and his business more successful.

Therefore, when launching a new service, the very first objective of services marketers is to establish at least three credible reference accounts that can be used as proof sources. This is of utmost importance and why the testing step is so important—so that you can start the race to new services sales running.

The second most common approach to getting decision-making information is to find it on the Internet. The good news is that the attributes of strong Web site design and search engine optimization are established. Providers of these services are abundant and the investment is manageable. The bad news is that the quantity of meaningful e-information on services is very limited, and the quality is usually lousy. Furthermore, searchers for information on services must jump through many hoops even to find anything. Don't believe me? Go to your Web site and try to find out what you can about the services your company offers.

The third most common approach should bring a smile to everyone who runs services in a product company, as they are readily sought out to share information on services. To make this effective, though, it means that the people on the product side of the house must have heard of your services, know what they are for, believe in their value, and are able to articulate their value. This means that along with promoting outside your company into the marketplace, you must promote inside your company as well.

We now know our three areas of emphasis. Let's talk about the vehicles we can use to be successful.

The left-hand side of Figure 23 shows how most services providers promote their offerings—a big emphasis on collateral and data sheets! On the right-hand side you see what the services marketers who "get it" do:

- *Do really good work.* When you first launch new services, everyone is watching you. Hence the criticality of doing whatever you can to get it right. That drives confidence and a willingness to tout your capabilities.
- *Reference/success stories.* Again, people will always believe their

Figure 23

Promoting: What Services Providers Are Doing versus What Works

WHAT DOING	WHAT WORKS
Collateral and data sheets	High-quality services experiences
More collateral and data sheets	Reference/success stories
Even more collateral and data sheets	E-newsletters
World Wide Web	World Wide Web
Direct mail	Seminars
Trade shows	PR
PR	Industry influencers briefings

Source: ITSMA Survey.

peers more than they will believe you. Focus on this principle.

- *Appropriate e-marketing.* Solid, informative, easy-to-use Web sites with quick access to testimonials, e-newsletters that focus on testimonials, and Webinars that ideally have your customers or other outside experts telling your story are key. All are inexpensive, relatively easy to do, and powerful in impact.
- *Face-to-face events.* These include seminars, briefings, or any way to get your best prospects to mingle with your best customers.

Step Nine: Sell

Now is the time to get everyone who touches the customer the training and tools necessary to sell your new services. This should be created based upon what was learned in the earlier eight steps. Since we are asking people to do new things, the best place to start is by using the performance management system discussed in Chapter 2 and adapting it to everyone responsible for influencing the customer.

1. *Fitting performance specifications.* For each of your customer-touching positions (pre-sales support, service account managers, dedicated services sellers, practice leaders, services managers, implementation consultants, field service engineers), you need to determine their selling roles and responsibilities, the process you want them to follow, and how they will interact with not only the customer but others in their organization, and partners, if applicable. Expectations should be established with specific measurable objectives put in place for each position.

   Depending on how big a change this is for your people, you may need to assess their willingness and ability to do what you want. You may need to scale down your expectations, vary your expectation by capability, or even shift some people into new roles.

2. *Adequate resources.* Your people need to have new information and tools, and possibly new skills to quickly adapt the new selling behaviors you want. The most effective and efficient way

to do this is through tailored training. Your training should include:

- The findings from the VOC research and the testing with reference accounts including:
    - What customers valued most.
    - How the new offerings address important customer needs.
    - How customers in the test phase responded.
- Sales tools developed from the findings:
    - Successful case study write-ups from reference accounts.
    - Feature-benefit profiles for all offerings focusing on the high-value benefits uncovered in the VOC.
    - ROI calculators to help your people help their customers in quantifying and justifying their decision to buy.
    - Anything else that will make them effective.
- Introduction or reinforcement of the selling skills needed and the selling approach to follow.
- Realistic practice sessions to help participants become competent in having successful conversations with customers and using the tools appropriately.
- Lots of discussions to help participants become comfortable and confident in their new selling behavior.

3. *Marketing activities.* Along with the training and selling tools for the people tasked with helping sell the new services, services marketers should do everything they can to make the selling process easier. This includes doing all the promoting activities listed in the last section: publishing success stories, regularly sending quality e-mails, having a Web site that puts services in the best light, speaking at and attending seminars, and hosting mixed groups of executives (both customers and prospects) both to start relationships and to allow your loyal customers to sell for you.

4. *Minimal interference.* There is nothing more discouraging to a motivated person than having management roadblocks get in the way of what they are supposed to do and want to do. If you want a field services engineer to spend four hours a week supporting

selling efforts, then remove several hours of something less important from his workload.

> GIST: Before you giveth, taketh away.

5. *Appropriate consequences.* Add incentives and disincentives that will make people do the right thing.
6. *Quality feedback.* Give people the performance information they need, when they need it.

Step Ten: Maximize Performance

At this step, you are ready to reap the harvest of your hard work. High-potential services have been developed, packaged, tested, and sold with a core group of customers who have bought them, like the results, and are telling the marketplace how valuable they are. In quality language, we are talking continuous improvement—fine-tuning offerings, streamlining processes, and simplifying how things get done. However, when we step back and look at all your services as a portfolio of services, they must be managed.

The Relentless Erosion
Figure 24 defines your services offerings from your customers' viewpoints. The X axis shows the degree of uniqueness of your offerings, and the Y axis demonstrates the importance of your offerings to the customer. Plot all your services on this chart using your VOC information and your experience as your guide. Hopefully, at least a few of your new offerings will fall into the upper right quadrant, being seen by your customers as both important and unique.

Overlaying this chart is the zone of competition, ranging from innovation to emulation, and finally, replication that demonstrates the law of relentless erosion.

Figure 24

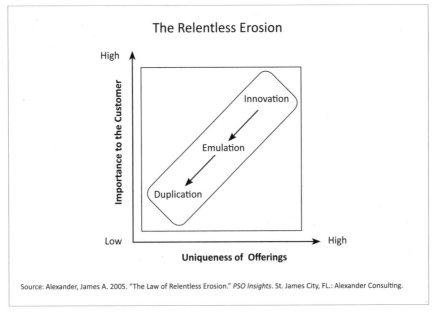

The Relentless Erosion

Source: Alexander, James A. 2005. "The Law of Relentless Erosion." *PSO Insights*. St. James City, FL.: Alexander Consulting.

Here is an example of how the law of relentless erosion works. Let's say that you've come up with a brand-new service that no one else in your market offers, and one that customers feel is important to their business. Congratulations, your competitors lustfully see your offering as the innovation that it is, but fortunately for you, they can do nothing about it for a while, leaving you with new and very profitable revenue. This is where you'd like all of your new services to start.

However, this time at the top doesn't last very long, as your best competitors immediately start to emulate you, trying their hardest to match your service to stem the tide of defections or hop on the bandwagon of growth that you've introduced. As customers gain experience about your service and your competitors' service, familiarity lessens perceived importance, and similar choices lower perceived uniqueness. Hence the slide down and to the left.

Finally, your competitors' reverse engineering is successful, and the code is broken. The secret sauce is now no longer secret, and your offering becomes ho-hum. Customers will still buy the service, but only if the cost is right and the hassles are few. You have just experienced the law of relentless erosion firsthand—taking a services offering from breakthrough to commodity in three simple steps!

So what can be learned from this?

1. *Accept the reality.* This is just Darwinian principles applied to business, so you are going to have to deal with it.
2. *Manage each phase differently.* During innovation, focus on aggressive sales. At the emulation point, target savvy marketing. And when replication hits, make efficient delivery the organizational mantra.
3. *Strive for balance.* Too many services organizations are overloaded at the commodity level. A healthy blend for your portfolio is a mix of one-third innovation, one-third emulation, and one-third replication.

> GIST: Avoid the irritation of the law of relentless erosion: Lead with innovation, finesse the emulation, and manage the imitation.

Best Practices

1. Put seasoned services marketers in charge of services marketing and make them accountable.
2. Start your marketing, selling, and delivering by building a value proposition appropriate to each customer.
3. Don't make offering decisions based upon best guesses; ground your decisions in the voice of the customer.
4. Manage your services portfolio by balancing offerings and continually replenishing the mix with new, innovative services.
5. Remember that everyone sells services. Give them the knowledge, skills, and tools to be successful.

Conclusion

The 10 steps to building high-value services offerings are well defined, doable, and effective. Followed in sequence, they will help you create a robust portfolio of services that will generate a new profitable revenue stream, and complement and enhance product sales as well.

Fast-Tracking Services Development

Don't get me wrong, I am a firm believer in following the 10 steps to profitably launching new services in almost any situation, but every now and then, it is not fast enough.

Figure 1

Fast-Tracking Services Offering Development

	Strongly Disagree			Strongly Agree	
1. Is the identified need known to be important to prospects?	1	2	3	4	5
2. Do prospects have a sense of urgency in addressing this need?	1	2	3	4	5
3. Are short-term benefits to us clear and worthwhile?	1	2	3	4	5
4. If there was a gun to our heads, could we launch the service immediately?	1	2	3	4	5
5. If there was a gun to their heads, could competitors launch similar services offerings immediately?	1	2	3	4	5
6. Is there strategic value to the services offering?	1	2	3	4	5

Figure 1 helps us determine when we should abandon the more rigorous 10-step approach to services offering development and go fast-track. Let me give you an example of how this works: I had a client whose customers just had an important requirement put in place by the government. In this case, the answer to question number one ("Is the identified need known to be important?") was a five on a five-point scale of importance, as non-compliance meant losing a big portion of their funding. The answer to question number two ("Do prospects have a sense of urgency in addressing this need?") was also a five in importance, as most of them felt the 120-day window was just about ridiculous. To my client, the answer to question number three ("Are short-term benefits to us clear and worthwhile?") was a four on the importance scale, as they knew their customers would be very willing to pay for just about anything they thought could help them meet this deadline. Initially, the client felt that the answer to question number four ("If there was a gun to our heads, could we launch the service immediately?") was a two. However, they eventually agreed that it could possibly be a four. They felt basically the same in answering question number five. There response to question six ("Is there strategic value to the services offering?") was a five in importance, as they felt this could reposition themselves in their marketplace and possibly help lead to long-term competitive advantage. So with a total score of 28 out of 30, it was worth the risk of fast-tracking.

In order to make fast-tracking work, however, four rules must be followed:

1. *Commit to a BHAG (big, hairy audacious goal).* In order to get people to think and act differently, they need a goal that they don't feel they could reach by doing business as usual.
2. *Forget sequence.* Do all major tasks in parallel. You don't have the luxury of a 1-2-3 approach; just do it.
3. *Good enough is good enough.* Don't allow perfectionists on the team. Once things meet minimum requirements, move on.
4. *Small is beautiful.* Empower a few folks for action (the crazier, the better).

GIST: When fast-tracking, avoid committees and large teams. Find a few smart folks who think differently, give them the BHAG, and get out of their way.

CHAPTER 6

The Challenge of the Channel

Organizations getting serious about selling services often must look to channel partners to help them accomplish their services objectives. However, under what circumstances is it a good idea to use channel partners for delivering services? How about selling services? How do you decide which types of services they should sell and/or deliver? As you build and broaden your services capabilities, what is the best way to deal with existing channel partners whose primary focus has been product sales? How do you minimize competition with existing channel partners who already offer the services you are building and planning to deploy? What are the appropriate criteria for selecting partners in situations where it makes no sense for you to go direct?

In this chapter you'll learn the obstacles present in building services channel partnerships and understand ways to think about services and the channel strategically, based upon your core and distinct competencies. You'll also find out more about the steps to establishing a strong services partnership model, and you'll learn how to use a tool to screen potential partners to evaluate the business fit. Finally, you'll discover the best practices in services channel partnership management.

Who Are Your Channel Partners?

Depending on your situation and the nomenclature used in your particular industry, your potential services channel partners might be called distributors, wholesalers, dealers, value-added resellers, manufacturer representatives, system integrators, consulting firms, independent services organizations, independent services providers, or in some cases, direct competitors. These channel partners may range from one-person shops to multinational corporations.

Furthermore, in some situations it makes sense to consider your customers as potential services channel partners if they have the capability and the desire to self-service your offerings themselves.

Traditional Use of Channel Partners

It is important to remember that in the majority of situations, companies first looked to channel partners to help them sell more products. Properly selected and managed, motivated channel partners helped companies sell more products cheaper and easier than they could do on their own. Your company's emphasis was in getting your channel partners capable of selling your products the way you wanted them sold and keeping them motivated to sell your offerings, and not your competitors' offerings.

Services Channel Partners

Services executives frequently identify effectively finding and managing services channel partners as one of the more difficult aspects of running the services business. Research of mine (see Figure 25) confirms this, revealing that services operations' biggest critical issue is dealing with channel challenges. This probably is not surprising to many of you. Research respondents specifically cited such concerns as two-tier distribution channel conflict, balancing disparate goals

Figure 25

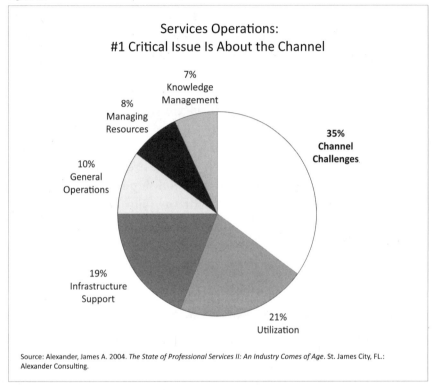

Services Operations:
#1 Critical Issue Is About the Channel

- 7% Knowledge Management
- 8% Managing Resources
- 10% General Operations
- 35% Channel Challenges
- 19% Infrastructure Support
- 21% Utilization

Source: Alexander, James A. 2004. *The State of Professional Services II: An Industry Comes of Age*. St. James City, FL.: Alexander Consulting.

between partners and the services organization, and sales channels that do not know how to or do not want to sell services.

Challenges of Finding and Keeping Strong Services Channel Partners

In considering the right services channel partners for your needs, several issues must be addressed.

Complexity

In some situations, your organization will be responsible for selling services, and all you need is a competent, reliable provider of services in a specific geography or industry. In other situations you may only be looking for someone to sell your services and you will deliver them. In still other situations you may want your services channel partner to both sell and deliver your services. Or you may want your channel partners to sell and/or deliver certain services but not others. Furthermore, you may prefer that the mix of services (start-up, uptime, or professional services) vary by geography, market, industry, or type of customer.

And of course your potential services channel partners will vary in their existing services capabilities, their desire to deliver services, and their motivation to sell services, depending upon their history, business strategy, goals, and opportunities. Furthermore, just like your organization, their capabilities, strategy, and motivation will also vary by industry and location.

GIST: Dozens of variables must be considered in your decision on how to sell and deliver services in different scenarios.

Reputation at Risk

In situations where you have a third party delivering your services, no matter what the name on the services provider's shirt, your customers think of them as an extension of your organization. Hence, customers relate a good service experience with your services channel partner to your organization, but they also hold your organization responsible if they are dissatisfied by channel partner performance. A few bad experiences from a few channel partners can have a major impact on the reputation of your services organization, and can negatively impact your company's overall brand.

GIST: Like it or not, your image is directly tied to the performance of your channel partners.

Maintaining Quality Control

Getting people to do what you want, how you want, and when you want is never simple, but it is much easier when they work directly for you. Getting people from another organization to consistently deliver services up to your standards is tough. This becomes an even bigger issue when you are trying to deliver a global service quality standard everywhere around the world using multiple channel partners. For example, it may be next to impossible to find any services channel partners in certain remote locations such as Sahara Africa, let alone assure the quality services performance of their actions. Furthermore, difficult terrain, extreme weather, and the customs and laws of some third-world countries add to unpredictability, high costs, and an increased probability of not achieving planned performance standards.

> GIST: Maintaining consistent quality around the globe is the Achilles' heel of the services executive.

Creating Competitors

When you introduce another organization to your business model, educate them on your products, and train them to effectively and efficiently sell and deliver your services offerings, you run the risk of creating a future competitor.

> GIST: Things change. Plan for the best, but prepare for the worst.

Sometimes you may not know who the customers are. If your organization has relied upon distribution to sell products in the past, you may not know who your end users are. The emphasis at that time was getting the resellers to first buy, and then sell, your products, and not much else mattered. The only service concerns your organization might have had were keeping warranty costs to a minimum and making sure the resellers were meeting minimum levels of customer satisfaction. Hence, your organization may never have seen the need to develop a database of the end users of your products.

GIST: Without an accurate database of your installed base, effectively selling and delivering services is almost impossible.

Existing Partners May Resist

Ponder Point: When you change the rules, expect lots of protest.

In finding services channel partners, you may first want to consider your existing channel partners as candidates because you already have a relationship with them, and your existing agreements may require involving them. In addition, you may get pressure from the sales organization to give this group the right of first refusal, as they want to do nothing that jeopardizes product sales.

Yet, remember that the focus of the majority of your existing channel partners was and is to sell products, period. The primary components of your agreements with them were all about product sales volume. This is what your organization has wanted and focused on, possibly for decades. Most of these partners have a product-centered culture (like your organization once had or currently has) and don't want to deal with services, as they see it as a distraction and a detriment to running their business. Hence, they will resist your overtures or requests or demands that they now build services capabilities and/or selling services competencies, as it is not in their DNA.

On the other extreme, though, within your existing channel partners you probably have a small number who have already recognized the value of services, and they currently sell and provide the services you are trying to expand into. In fact, in the past, your organization may have encouraged these channel partners to aggressively build and sell services independently, as your company had no interest in services at that time. Therefore, this select few of your existing channel partners will now see you as trying to compete with them for "their customers." Of course they will resist your advances, as they perceive that you are now changing the rules and trying to move into their turf.

Here is an example: Back in the "good old days" a client of my organization sold, through resellers, a highly profitable proprietary product to the tune of roughly $300,000 per box. A few start-up services were "thrown in" to secure the sale and make sure the box performed as required. Since the product addressed mission-critical functions, uptime services were easily sold and delivered by our client, again at envious profit margins. If the customer had any other needs "beyond the box," the reseller took care of them by providing professional services. Never mind that these "additional needs" often amounted to seven figures. Roles were clean and straightforward. Profitable growth was relatively easy and predictable. Life was good.

Over just a few years, however, the former $300,000 proprietary product evolved into a $30,000 open system box competing against a plethora of cheaper choices. The once-easy uptime services sale became not so easy, since products were more reliable, and similar, "just-as-good" uptime services were being offered at lower prices, putting pressure on profit margins. So our client decided that its only hope of growing the business at acceptable levels of profitability, aside from acquiring or being acquired or dramatically altering the business focus, lies in expanding into professional services. It appeared to be a challenging, but doable task. But wait...professional services businesses are built upon strong client trust, and trust is centered upon relationships. In this case, the reseller still owned the client relationship. In order to advance the professional services initiative, our client had to invest the time to create new customer relationships, aggressively compete for account control, and manage conflict on several fronts, as former "partners" now viewed our client not only as a competitor, but as a two-faced, turncoat, back-stabbing competitor. This was a very difficult situation that never reached the hope-for goal.

> GIST: On the one hand, the majority of your existing partners flat out don't want to sell services or provide services. On the other hand, you have a few existing partners (usually some of your best) that now see you as wanting to compete with them. Of course they will feel both protective and possibly frightened at your new services strategy. Getting their cooperation is a tough challenge.

To add fuel to the fire, some of your existing channel partners have been providing services for free, bringing to bear the special "free to fee" challenges brought out in Chapter 4.

More on how to address these challenges a little later.

Using Services to Build Distinct Competencies

Ponder Point: You can only do a few things well.

In this section you'll learn how services can best support the organization strategy by expanding necessary core competencies and creating new, distinct competencies that can lead to competitive advantage. Understanding the model presented will help you make better choices in selecting the right channel partners.

Core Is Good

For years strategists have urged executives to "keep to your core," "stick to your knitting," define what you can do really well and try to outsource everything else. As long as the core is directed toward meeting key customer expectations, this is solid advice that has helped many organizations redirect their resources and fine-tune their focus to extract both efficiency and effectiveness internally.

The lesson here for services is that as customers' needs and wants expand (and they always do), services capabilities help support and enhance your technology and product core. Having some core services offerings is expected by your customers and is necessary to complete a portfolio of offerings. Properly managed, core services can provide an acceptable margin of profitability and are often seen as the table stakes in a competitive industry, required to help protect the business from competitors that may also be expanding their services offerings.

This is all well and good, but it is not enough. The downside is that often your core competency is the same as your top competitor's core competency. So unless your core competency is seen as markedly better externally (in your customers' eyes, not yours), you have no marketplace differentiation, zip advantage, zero uniqueness. In other words, your organization's offerings will be seen as commodities.

Distinct Is Better

The key to marketplace uniqueness is not core competencies, but distinct competencies—capabilities or organizational attributes that make your company clearly superior to your competitors in things that customers care about (hence, they will pay for them). Distinct competencies are what strategy is all about. Ideally, distinct competencies are difficult and/or time-consuming to imitate (e.g., patents, proprietary industry benchmarks/best-practice data, exclusive agreements, powerful brands). Therefore, they build barriers to entry, dissuading potential newcomers from targeting your market and preventing existing competitors from copying your approach, as the potential value is outweighed by the high cost of time and effort. True distinct competencies yield more, better, and easier sales, as well as the profitable growth that results. From a big-picture perspective, business focus should strongly favor the development, growth, expansion, and protection of your distinct competency, as it is the secret sauce, the get-out-of-jail-free card, the force field that protects organization sustainability.

Depending on the maturity of your industry, the complexity of your customers' issues, the sophistication, importance, and cost of your products, and the strategy of your competitors, different services capabilities offer opportunities for distinction. For example, in some product companies, just having a viable services capability that your competitors don't offer can provide differentiation that is important to customers, thus greatly increasing the probability of more product sales and more services sales.

If your competitors offer services, they may not be able to provide those services regionally or nationally or globally. If you have the appropriate amount of density and ability to scale, you have an advantage. If you are able to ensure that customers receive levels of uptime higher than your competitors can provide through your robust services level agreements, this will get you more sales of both products and services. Having dedicated services account managers assigned to key accounts directly influences contract renewals and overall account sales, and creates reference accounts that help gain other new business. Having strong services horsepower as a part of a pre-sales team can add credibility to your company and help craft stronger recommendations that improve win rates. Offering remote monitoring, diagnosing, and fixing capabilities may help your customers avoid problems and give you a big cost savings over competitors who must rely on field services to fix the same problems.

Offering multivendor services, being willing and able to service competitor and, potentially, other non-competitive products, may also set you apart from others. It can simplify your customers' lives while adding revenue and building an on-site presence that can lead to the removal of all competitive products over time. Because all solutions are services-led, in-depth professional services may allow a business to have a true solutions capability, gaining a larger share of customers' wallets while building executive-level bonds that resist competitive inroads.

If you are able to teach and motivate your customers to do their own maintenance, troubleshooting, and repair, this might be a strong enticement for them to choose your organization over others. For many services organizations, however, the best chance for distinction is in creating a superior reputation for relentless reliability—doing it right the first time, every time. In a world where customers often describe solutions implementation as "hit or miss," "always a gamble," "geez, I hope they get it right," a services brand of utter dependability offers incredible promise that is quite appealing to reluctant or downright scared customers.

On the flip side, if your organization does not have robust services capabilities, you are not only missing out on profitable growth and competitive differentiation, but you are also making yourself vulnerable to competitive threats.

Figure 26 expands on the distinctness of your capabilities by adding the importance of the capabilities of your organization to the mix. This model can provide your organization with a handy tool

Figure 26

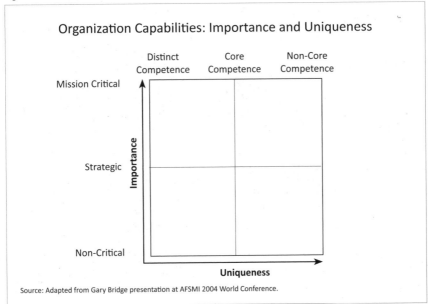

Source: Adapted from Gary Bridge presentation at AFSMI 2004 World Conference.

to identify and compare your capabilities and attributes by value, defined as the degree of uniqueness and organization importance; to simplify, the higher up and farther to the left, the greater the value. Furthermore, understanding where your services land on this model will have a direct bearing on when and where you want to use services channel partners.

Figure 27 expands on Figure 26, outlining the appropriate strategy based upon the uniqueness and distinctiveness of your organizational capabilities and the products and services that are spawned by them.

Retain In-House

Capabilities that are mission-critical, and in which you have distinct competency, are your crown jewels. These capabilities should be retained, nurtured, kept in-house, and guarded under lock and key. For example, a distinct, mission-critical services offering that no one else can provide would be plotted up and to the left in this figure.

Figure 27

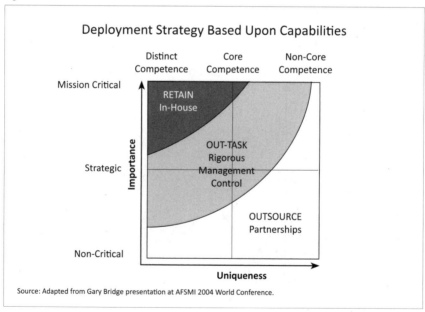

Source: Adapted from Gary Bridge presentation at AFSMI 2004 World Conference.

Since the creation and delivery of these services are often dependent on a small number of brilliant people, it would be prudent to provide lots of incentives to keep them motivated, and golden handcuffs to keep them on board.

Another example of a capability that should be retained in-house might be a unique, smart technology that your company owns outright that allows you to remotely fix software issues dramatically cheaper and faster than your competitors. Obviously, this software should not be licensed, and access to the source code and vital innards should be tightly controlled. Again, the really smart folks behind it should be retained at all costs. In these scenarios, you would never take the risk to depend on channel partners or anyone else to deliver these capabilities.

Outsource
On the other extreme (down and to the right on Figure 27) are capabilities and services offerings that you don't have today nor want to provide in the future (although you could easily do it). The appropriate strategy here is to create partnerships and outsource the task to companies that specialize in them. Since these tasks are low on the importance scale, your organization should not spend much time dealing with them. Contracts should be crafted outlining expectations, and then the day-to-day management should be left to the third party. All sorts of things fall into this arena, from outsourcing janitorial services to human resource benefit packages to IT departments. From a services-business perspective, examples of non-critical functions worthy of outsourcing consideration might include travel planning for your consultants and field engineers, depot repair for a low-priced commodity product, or Web site development and support for self-services.

Out-Task
The middle grouping is where consideration of services channel partners comes into play. Although you have the capabilities to sell and/or deliver these important services, your resources might pro-

vide higher value if used elsewhere. In this case, if you find a suitable match, you would out-task these services to a services channel partner, but manage them rigorously.

For example, your organization might have the ability in-house, but decide for financial considerations to out-task field services operations in the Asia Pacific region to a services channel partner. Or in a similar situation, you may want to have direct field personnel in all the major metropolitan areas of North America, but choose to use services channel partners everywhere else. Another variation might be for your organization to sell and provide your entire services portfolio to enterprise accounts while using channel partners in the commercial space.

Another example is that, although you could do it very well, you may find that out-tasking all contact centers is the best choice for your situation. Again, these are important capabilities that you certainly could handle, but from a resource and focus perspective, your organization might be better served by targeting, building, and enhancing distinct services competencies that are vital to your organization's success.

The concept of core and distinct competencies is a central tenet of organizational effectiveness. Services have the potential to significantly shift the balance from core to distinguished. Mission-critical, unique services capabilities should be kept in-house, financed, and nurtured. Strategic services capabilities that are not distinctive should be out-tasked to services channel partners and rigorously managed to deliver high-quality, consistent customer results. Non-critical, undifferentiated services should be farmed out to other partners to run under well-defined services level agreements.

Steps to Selecting, Building, and Maintaining Strong Services Channel Partners

Obviously, addressing the "challenge of the channel" requires a strong, well-thought-out approach. Following are 10 steps to help you find, motivate, and retain the right services channel partners.

1. Use the capabilities strategy model to plot your existing services and solutions. I include solutions here, as services are a vital solutions component and are important to the business strategy according to your competence status and importance to your company. Voice of the customer findings (see Chapter 5), competitive intelligence reports, industry trends, and internal strategy documents are all potential inputs to accurately completing this model. Don't be dismayed if you don't have many offerings way up and way left on the chart.

2. As part of your services business plan, create a "plan for distinction" outlining what is needed to maintain your status for those extremely important and highly unique services in place today, and what is needed (e.g., new skills and knowledge required, alliances created, systems developed) to develop more offerings that are unique and important that can help achieve competitive advantage in the future.

   Examples might include recruiting and hiring top-notch services account managers with strong business acumen, or investing more in advancing remote technologies, or aggressively pursuing multivendor opportunities. Since this is the most important part of the services business, assign your best managers and top talent to lead and implement these innovative projects and key customer engagements. Of course resources need to be reallocated from other less valuable projects to support this strategic initiative. And remember, capabilities and services that fall into the "retain in-house" category are not candidates for channel partners of any kind.

3. At the other extreme, all tasks falling into the non-critical, non-core category should be outsourced as quickly as possible to external partners who can do these functions easier, faster, and cheaper. With guidelines from services management, a support function such as procurement should assume responsibility to find and regulate appropriate partners. Services should not get involved again unless core metrics are not being met that have

a negative impact on the services organization. The talents of channel partners should not be required here either.

4. Using all the projections, plans, and insights available, start to think through how you'll deal with strategic services issues where you possess core services competencies but may need to consider out-tasking. The goal is to best focus your internal capabilities to gain the most leverage and then balance them off with help from select services channel partners.

List the services capabilities needed to deliver on your current services commitments and probable future engagements. Then think through your existing capabilities and how well they align. Of course cost, timeliness, and quality are always factors of consideration.

For example, if you are being required to provide professional services for all of Germany, you may desire to expand your internal capabilities to cover those needs by hiring people and adding necessary infrastructure. However, if you also need to provide uptime services in Latin America, you may feel that it makes the most sense to use services channel partners. Review needs by geographies, industries, market segments, and strategic accounts. Think through the three types of services—start-up, uptime, and professional services—that might come into play. Finally, analyze all the people, process, and technical requirements needed to deliver on each need.

5. After best determining where services channel partners would be most beneficial, develop a criteria screen for prospective services channel partners to objectively determine the probability of success.

Figure 28 is an example of how my organization helped a client develop a criteria screen for searching for services channel partners. Our client was selling and servicing their products directly to all customers in the major metropolitan areas in North America, but wanted a partner or partners to deliver adequate-quality, low-cost field services coverage everywhere else. Here is a succinct explanation of each of the factors included in this

Figure 28

Services Channel Partner Criteria Screen – EXAMPLE –					

CRITERIA		RATING			
	Low				*High*
1. Services Capabilities	1	2	3	4	5
2. Partnership Attitude	1	2	3	4	5
3. Non-Competitive	1	2	3	4	5
4. Marketplace Credibility	1	2	3	4	5
5. Sales Capabilities	1	2	3	4	5
6. Geographic Coverage	1	2	3	4	5
7. Cost Model	1	2	3	4	5
8. Technology Fit	1	2	3	4	5

criteria screen that we developed together:

- *Services capabilities.* They wanted an organization that had competence in their technology and similar products so that minimal training would be required.
- *Partnership attitude.* Having had bad partner experiences in the past, they wanted to make sure that whomever they worked with had a win-win philosophy going into the relationship.
- *Non-competitive.* It was a requirement that their partners did not and would not service competitive products or compete against them in their major cities.
- *Marketplace credibility.* It wasn't necessary that their chosen partner was seen as an industry star, but they wanted to make sure they were seen as reputable.
- *Sales capabilities.* Although not a must-have, ideally they wanted an organization that could not only service their products, but sell all their services.
- *Geographic coverage.* This was a big one. They required partners that had enough resources (feet on the street) to be able to meet their service level agreement metrics even in remote areas.

- *Cost model.* They desired a company that was lean enough to charge a competitive price while allowing both their company and the partner to make a decent profit margin.
- *Technology fit.* They were hoping for partners with similar technology platforms so that communications and reporting would not require major system integration.

This criteria screen proved invaluable in finding the best partners for this long-term engagement.

Determine the factors that are most important to your unique situation, define them, and weigh them accordingly. You will then have a common standard from which to objectively consider services channel partner choices.

Build, Borrow, or Buy Capabilities

Many executives who want to get their companies into services quickly have to come to grips with either building capabilities, borrowing capabilities (e.g., services channel partners), or buying existing services companies. Of course, there are plusses and minuses to all three options. When helping our clients shape and create services strategies, we often suggest that while building core internal capabilities and examining partner choices they search out potential acquisition candidates, as this can be the fastest way make an industry impact. Acquisitions also take away the threat of creating future competitors. Once again, one of your first steps is building a criteria screen to define what a good acquisition looks like.

---

6. Do initial research to find possible prospects. Talk to industry people in the know to get initial information and disqualify poor fits. Follow this up with online research. Note that if it is important to keep your search confidential, use others to act as your

representatives to front the search until it is appropriate for non-disclosures and serious face-to-face meetings.

7. Romance your prospects. Just like dealing with a customer or prospect, when it looks like a potentially good fit, learn their issues and needs. Take the time to think about what it is you bring to the table that they would value. New, profitable revenue? Probably. A chance to work with an industry heavyweight? Possibly. If times are tough, a way to make their expensive resources sitting on the bench billable? Absolutely. Your goal is to get them excited enough to take your solicitation seriously.

8. Schedule an initial face-to-face meeting early on to test business fit and relationship potential. Yes, initially conversations can be held over the phone, but forming a partnership is too important not to meet in person.

Start by sharing the potential benefits to be gained by your chosen partner in terms they care about, and then confirm that these benefits are important to them. Next, share your criteria screen, clearly explaining the meaning behind each factor and stating what are "musts" and what are "wants." Ask your prospective partner what defines a good partnership from their perspective. If things are positive at this point, share some potential low-hanging fruit that they will probably be able to take advantage of quickly. Nothing is better than bringing new business to a new partnership, as it demonstrates trust and commitment. This is especially important when you will be asking your partner to invest time and money.

At this point in the face-to-face meeting, address the potential stumbling blocks to the relationship and jointly determine how they should be handled. It is good to give this some thought and have these prepared ahead of time. Example issues to be addressed include:

- How will we both make money?
- How will risk be shared?
- What investments are needed and who will make them?
- Who will own the customer relationship?

- What metrics should we use to judge success?
- What is our communications and change management plan for sustaining the relationship?
- Who will handle inquiries and leads?
- What about spinoffs from other-than-core areas?
- What role should outside advisors play in the process in order to keep it fair and moving along?
- What is the exit strategy?

9. If the initial meetings go well, there is strong interest on both sides, and by all indications it looks like a good fit, then develop a draft agreement addressing all the issues listed in the previous steps, and any others that arise, in enough detail so that all is crystal-clear.

What If Your Organization Is the Potential Services Channel Partner?

If your organization is a potential services provider, the steps outlined above and the best practices described below are all relevant to you. Build your own distinct competencies, create criteria screens, understand what your potential services partners want and need, and then aggressively go after them. Many, many services organizations are in need of good partners, and it might as well be you.

---

10. While the agreement is being negotiated, develop an integrated marketing plan. First, determine what message will be communicated internally to the services organization, sales, and everyone else. Communicate what you've done, why you've done it, and the benefits to the organization. Be sure to let people whose jobs are impacted know their new expectations.

   After the internal communication process is completed, a marketing campaign should be developed for all external organizations that might be impacted, including your current installed base, prospects, and other organizations. Again, following the simple model of stating what you've done, why you've done it, and the benefit to the specific stakeholder you are addressing will get the job done effectively.

Best Practices in Services Channel Management

1. *Assign a senior person to manage all services channel partnerships, with specific measurable goals and metrics.* Just as with any other important task, one individual needs to be both responsible and accountable.
2. *Develop and consistently use clearly defined partnership criteria.* This will help to quantify the intangible and qualify the organizations most likely to be successful.
3. *Involve your key executives in the services channel partner selection process.* The success of your services channel partners impacts the success of your entire company. Hence, to get and keep executives on board, involve them in the process.
4. *Use an outside services industry expert to help craft and lead the confidential partnership search.* The right person(s) will bring not only services and industry knowledge that will focus the search, but also a professional, non-biased approach to smooth and speed the selection process.
5. *Give choices to your existing channel partners.* As described earlier, many of them are mainly product-sales driven. Don't demand that they change their spots, however, explain the growth and profit opportunities available to them if they are willing to invest and amend their business charter. If they choose not to, sharing your services story and giving them the chance to participate lessens their concerns when you become more involved in the services side of "their customers" or when you assign a new services channel partner to create and fill new services demands.
6. *Require services providers to demonstrate their competence to you be-*

fore turning them loose. Remember that from the customer's stand-point, they are you, so don't let them touch your customers or your prospects until they can do what you want them to do, the way you want it done. Charge them for the necessary training because it has value and is a requirement of the agreement. If your agreement with a services provider requires that they sell the services as well, their sellers need to demonstrate selling services proficiency before they visit the first customer.

7. *Differentiate the level of your services channel partners' expectations, and reward them accordingly.* For example, services channel partners that make big investments in hiring new talent and create a new infrastructure to support your new joint-channel goals deserve to be treated better than their less-committed peers. This superior treatment might result in a "Gold" status rating and entitle them to receive your best pricing, access to internal experts, and the opportunity to work with more lucrative accounts. Partners committing less might be on a "Silver" level, and those providing minimum levels of services investment might be classified as "Bronze."

   Furthermore, if the need is there, you might need to be creative and form a master services provider agreement with a uniquely qualified organization. For example, a reliable organization that takes on the entire realm of your services needs for you across Southern Europe or all of Latin America could be extremely valuable to you. Of course, that relationship might have a very different set of expectations and compensation plans. Be innovative when the situation demands.

8. *Require an annual certification audit.* Review all aspects of the services channel partner performance against standards, capability requirements, and goals. Use these findings to assign the classifications assigned above for the upcoming year. And, yes, you should charge for this as well. Or at least establish a value if you decide to do it for no charge.

9. *Never give up ownership of the customer.* Build alliances, create synergies, and capitalize on distinctive strengths, but judiciously

nurture and jealously guard your customer relationships—they are the heart, and the primary asset, of any services business.

10. *Treat your services channel partners as you would a key account.* Put an emphasis on sustaining the relationship, and proactively work to build and maintain trust. In a partnership, absence does not make the heart grow fonder—it often creates mistrust. Meet frequently in person to review mutual performance and work out issues before they become problems.

Conclusion

In the complex world of services, no one can go it alone. It takes reliable, capable, trustworthy services channel partners to meet global demands. There are many challenges to be dealt with, but following a proven approach will greatly improve your probability of forming mutually beneficial relationships that will drive your services success.

CHAPTER 7

Stranger in a Strange Land:
Five Steps to Services Leadership in a Product-Centric Company

You are the person responsible for making services successful within your product company—just how do you do it? What is required to change the perception of the services executive from the leader of the leper camp to that of a peer at the executive council? How do you effectively deal with a product culture that fights acceptance of services? Most importantly, how do you survive long enough to reach your services goals?

This chapter is specifically written for the services executive, the services champion designated to make the services organization successful inside of its product company parent in spite of the special challenges mentioned throughout the book thus far. The content is most relevant for those 80% of services leaders attempting to implement the product enhancement strategy ("have your cake and eat it too") described in Chapter 1. You will learn how to lead and manage through the five steps of the services life cycle: Analyze, Revise, Survive, Thrive, and Evangelize. You'll be introduced to the critical issues and priorities of each of the five steps and you'll learn how to effectively deal with each one. Finally, you'll discover the best practices required of a true services champion.

Ponder Point: Successfully leading a services organization in a product-centric company is not for the faint of heart. Learn what works.

Step One: Analyze

Just the facts, ma'am, just the facts.*

Whether you are in the throes of a startup or your services organization has been around since the days of analog, you must have facts to effectively run your business. Ideas, hunches, and past experience can get you by for a time if you are lucky, but current hard data drives decisions and, in the end, finalizes your fate.

The right information is especially important if you are the "Stranger" in the organization—the head of services in a product-centric world. If this is the case, you continually must justify your value, as well as your very existence. Credible information is the prime component of creating your services business case and building your personal credibility. Quality information will help you:

1. *Improve your services business.* By better understanding your highest-potential customers and discovering your highest-potential offerings, you can fill priority gaps and direct your capabilities where they will create the biggest impact.

2. *Enhance business alignment.* A deeper understanding of the marketplace and the key stakeholders in your company can help you better align your services organization with the overall business strategy and better contribute to accomplishing your mission.

3. *Build personal credibility.* Believe me, you will gain the most respect when dealing with your product peers and the product-thinking folks who run your outfit by making your points through credible data. Ranting and raving, pleading and praying have their place, but most of the time they don't do much for building esteem. Let the information make your case by showing the best value proposition for the business.

So, wherever your services organization is on the maturity scale, a must-do is a regularly scheduled annual assessment. Here is what you need to know, track, and base decisions upon:

1. Outside:
   - What your top customers want, need, and expect.
   - How you stack up against your best competitors.
   - What your services organization's brand awareness and brand quality are.
2. Inside:
   - How well your internal capabilities match marketplace needs and global best practices.
   - Perceptions of your services organization from the product, sales, product marketing, and senior management teams.

Three methods are the most appropriate for getting information from inside your company.

1. *Interviews.* The tried-and-true method of one-on-one, face-to-face interviews with the key players in the organization is a must. Develop a core group of questions you will ask everyone, yet leave room for plenty of expansion—you want people to tell you what they think, and why.
2. *Focus groups.* A second, less-used approach is focus groups. Done correctly, you can gather a lot of good information fast. However, bring in an outsider highly skilled at facilitation to gain the most benefit and avoid internal squabbles.
3. *Surveys.* A simple survey aimed at the people inside the services organization and others in the company (such as product sales and marketing) can yield good quantitative information. Here are some examples of comments you might hear:
   - *Product Salesperson:* "Giving services away helps me close deals."
   - *Technical Consultant:* "I see lots of opportunities on-site at the clients, but I don't know what to do about them."
   - *Corporate Marketing:* "We have a professional services group?"

See what I mean?

For a small investment in time, the information you will learn can help you improve. More important, though (and assuming you act upon their suggestions), is that by involving people in thinking about the issues of your services organization, they are already buying in to future changes. This is a critical cornerstone of change management—and change management is a critical skill of all Strangers.

Looking outside, there are numerous ways to gather marketplace information and a few key ones have already been referenced in earlier chapters. Bob Yopko, former vice president of global services for Emerson Electric and now a senior consultant at Alexander Consulting, believes in using customers to sell the rest of the organization: "Executives will question your views, but it is pretty hard for them to vote against what their best customers say they need. Use the voice of the customer to build your business case for services."

So invest the effort to get the facts—credible, real-time, in-depth information with the stakeholders that mean the most to the fate of your services organization. Many things will be confirmed. A few important surprises will arise. Involvement will build understanding for your services organization's issues and build your credibility as a services leader and executive peer. This is the first important step in leading a services organization in a product-dominant company.

> **GISTS: Remember: Get the facts, all the facts.**

Step Two: Revise

Once you have the relevant, in-depth, current information about key customers, the marketplace, your services personnel, and other key people inside your organization,

1. Analyze
2. Revise
3. Survive
4. Thrive
5. Evangelize

it is time to rethink, reformulate, and revise your services business and your personal leadership plans to test the probability of accomplishing your business goals.

Take a Reality Check

As a smart executive armed with the new, relevant information from your data gathering, the first thing you need to do is take another look at your goals for your services organization. Are they appropriate based upon what you now know? Realistically, is your mission attainable? Where can you expect resistance within the organization?

A SWOT Analysis, as seen in Figure 29, is a good tool to help organize your assessment data and answer these questions. It quickly (it takes about 30 minutes) can help you grasp where you are in relationship to accomplishing your services organization mission and identify the factors that can help you or hinder you in accomplishing

Figure 29

SWOT Analysis Transitioning from Product-Centered to Services-Led – EXAMPLE –	
Strengths	**Weaknesses**
• Strong customer reputation. • Strong technical people. • Executives aware of services potential.	• Product culture. • Company in cut-back mode. • No services infrastructure.
Opportunities	**Threats**
• No product competitors selling services. • Customers more sophisticated. • Independent services providers making inroads.	• Poor economy. • New technologies. • Fluctuating currencies.

your services goals.

Here's how you do it: First, using the information gathered in Step One, you (or you and your team) categorize your data internally as either strengths or weaknesses related to accomplishing your goals, and externally as either opportunities or threats. If you've been honest with yourself, you are now facing your current reality, however satisfying or unpleasant it may be. It may confirm the "do-ability" of your mission or cause you to make some adjustments. Either way, next you will need to find ways to leverage internal strengths and external opportunities while eliminating or minimizing internal weaknesses and external threats. Revisit this tool at least every six months to take the pulse of your change efforts.

The revelations of completing a services SWOT Analysis can be quite impactful. For instance, a recently hired vice president of professional services in a hardware company had this to say after completing this exercise in one of my transitioning to services workshops: "You know, it just isn't going to work. When you look at all the factors working against me, there is no way that this box company is ever going to be services-led. I'm going to have to change my approach or get my resume up to date!"

This was tough to swallow at the time, but better then, rather than later! She was able to lower her sights and develop a much less aggressive plan that was more appropriate to her current situation. Instead of sailing off into a storm that promised very big waves, she battened down the hatches and waited for the tide of opportunity to rise.

Build an Appealing Case for Change

Once you have confirmed or adjusted an appropriate and attainable mission for your services organization, you need to make it appealing—appealing enough to the key stakeholders inside and outside the company so that they will consider changing their behavior. As all the Strangers out there know, this can be challenging.

To align the information so that it will have the highest probability of being accepted by the key stakeholders, you first need to have a good understanding of both their business issues and their personal issues. I recommend a simple yet powerful tool to do this: the Stakeholder Analysis (Figure 30). Stakeholders are those who have a "stake" (something to win or lose) in whatever you are proposing or promoting or promising.

1. First, identify all the main players (stakeholders) who might be impacted by your ideas and determine their roles (the SWOT Analysis will help). Depending on factors such as your issues and the size of your organization, this could range from six to 60 people. In Figure 30, I list only three stakeholders to give you an idea of how it works.

2. Next, determine their business issues. In this case, the CEO was most concerned about regaining market leadership and thwarting new competitive threats. The CFO was (no surprise here) mainly concerned about cost control and shrinking profit margins. The vice president of sales was concerned about hitting his high-growth target, period.

3. Third, examine their personal issues. In this case, the CEO took pride in being known as an innovative leader. The CFO wanted

Figure 30

	Stakeholder Analysis – EXAMPLE –		
STAKEHOLDER	ROLE	BUSINESS ISSUES	PERSONAL ISSUES
John Smith CEO	Decision Maker	Regain market leadership. New competitive threats.	Recognition as an innovator.
Mary Jones CFO	Influencer	Cost control. Shrinking profit margins.	Demonstrate prowess.
Bill Adams VP Sales	Influencer	Hitting sales target.	"Looking good."

to broaden her influence in the organization, as the CEO would be retiring in two years, and she wanted to make a name for herself to be positioned as the heir apparent. Hence, anything that demonstrated her prowess would be of interest to her. The vice president of sales considered himself not only an expert in sales, but also in marketing, strategy, the industry, just about everything! What was important to him was that he looked good to anyone and everyone.

4. With all of the above done, you now can think through what you will want to communicate to each key stakeholder, and how you will want to communicate it. Just looking at the three stakeholders above, you'll quickly see that presenting the same message the same way to all three is a plan of disaster—the best you could do is one out of three, and this isn't baseball. Each individual needs to be treated as an individual, and your ideas must address their unique issues, showing them how they can benefit on both a business and a personal level. They don't have to be lengthy, but you need an individual plan of influence for each key stakeholder.

One of the most important aspects of this tool is that it forces you to think through all of the people who might be impacted by your plans. Many times, it is much broader than you originally thought. Furthermore, the first time you complete one of these analyses, you probably will find some gaps. It will force you to do some homework. It also will take the investment of a few hours (sometimes a day or two), but it is well worth it, as it greatly will improve your odds of success. And in the challenging role of a services leader in a product company, you should use all the tools you can get your hands on.

Energize through Involvement

A cardinal enabler of getting people to accept and embrace change is involving them in the process. Nothing works better. So look at all your key stakeholders and think about ways you can involve them. This involvement pays off big time when you go back to the customers you have involved in your research and tell them what you are doing and why. In many cases they are ready to buy, mainly because they helped contribute to the process.

The same is true, and may be even more important, as you try to influence your product peers and superiors in your company. Remember that what makes perfect sense to you may well appear alien to others in your organization. You'll remember that Step One emphasized personal interviews and focus groups of internal personnel. Doing these data-gathering activities not only yields good information, but it also sets the stage for buy-in.

Here is another very powerful involvement approach: Have the management team wrestle with the data—problem solving, coming up with options, determining the strengths and weaknesses of each choice, and reaching agreement through collaboration. Correctly done, this is a vehicle for accelerating positive change and advancing your services agenda.

Tony Pajk, president of Branson Ultrasonics, was faced with a tough task. He saw the need to aggressively move his company into services, but most of the players on his executive team were blinded by their current business success. Following my advice, he decided to do a global voice of the customer project to better understand the services potential and the best places to focus. To get his execs on board, he required all of them (including himself) to be involved in conducting the key account interviews, then analyzing the information and sharing it with their peers at a two-day services blueprinting session. This is what Tony had to say:

> *My team was very skeptical about services in the beginning; most felt our current efforts were effective. Nor were they very optimistic about customer reception to the interview process. However, the impact was remarkable. Sitting face-to-face with key accounts and not talking about products, but listening to the customers' business issues and organizational problems was very powerful and enlightening. They came to the blueprinting session highly energized and wanting to speak up for the customers they heard! They put aside their past biases and worked together to create a*

doable services plan. This was the turning point of truly getting the services buy-in at Branson and reinforcing our message to our customers that we were more than a product company—we were a total life cycle solutions company.

The step of Revise is all about using information to take a hard look at your services business and personal leadership plan, making realistic changes, and taking the right actions to get key folks on board to help you accomplish your goals.

GIST: Implementing the step of Revise is about the difference between being skeptically viewed as a Stranger or being admired as a unique contributor who makes everyone in the organization more successful.

Step Three: Survive

With your services business plan and your personal leadership blueprint in hand, it is time to do first things first, which is doing the basic requirements needed to survive as a services leader in a product-driven company and buying some time while building core capabilities. Here are the vital few mindsets and behaviors necessary to keep you on the payroll.

Recognize the Reality

You can't fight City Hall. East is east and west is west, and never the twain shall meet. You can call a duck a chicken, but it will still waddle and quack. In other words, you have to face the facts: You clearly may know the huge potential of your organization becoming a high-powered, services-led enterprise, but if you live in a product-thinking, product-acting, products-are-everything company, it isn't going to happen (at least for a while). So soften your speeches and mind your manners. You are going to have to live with it until the winds of change start to blow in a direction that makes your senior management willing to navigate a new course.

This is, by far, the most difficult element of being a Stranger in a Strange Land; you see the Promised Land, yet are stuck on the path of less potential with people who don't perceive the services vision. Patience, patience, patience is the difficult yet practical remedy.

Liz Murphy, vice president of professional services for Datatel, an ERP software company for higher education, had the personal goal of transforming her company into a services-push, product-follow organization. She readily saw the potential and embarked on an internal "let's change the company" crusade that was being resisted at every twist and turn. Her drive and her energy were being turned into frustration and despondency. She summed it up this way:

> Once I came to grips that my vision for service was just not possible at this time, it was like a big weight was taken from my shoulders. When I went from trying to change a resistant world to concentrating on what I could control, the disappointment and sense of doom went away.

Sounds like good advice, don't you think?

Create the Core

Whether a sports team, an army, or a business, you always need "strength up the middle," a core group upon which you can depend when trouble brews or opportunity bubbles. Important in any situation, this concept is vital in the early days of a services organization start-up. So put a major focus on defining/finding/developing a core leadership team—the project and practice leaders who will manage your consultants and engagements.

When reflecting upon the success he achieved starting up professional services at RSA Security, Rick Welch, former vice president of professional services, had this to say:

> *These people are really hard people to find, but they represent about 80% of your risk. They are doing the bidding, managing, and dealing with the tough issues. You need people who have been there. Of course, you will want to tap any existing talent, but you will have to go outside for some core experience. You will make enough mistakes on the tough situations; you don't need to make mistakes on the easy ones.*

So make creating the core a priority. Define the capabilities you need, aggressively go after them, and don't quit until you find the handful of highly talented people who will help you drive success.

Train the Team

Everyone, including you, needs ongoing training to increase knowledge, improve skills, and keep the right mindset. We all know that. But every day I run into situations with consultants who have never been trained in consulting and project managers who don't understand project definitions or scope creep. Budget, plan, and require that everyone update their skills, but focus on these three: project management, consulting skills, and selling capabilities. Make sure that:

- The training is high quality, services-specific, and tailored to the needs of your services organization. This is not the time to be on the cheap.
- The trainers not only know training, but they also understand the services business. Most don't.
- You have a plan to reinforce the training. If you don't, much of what is learned in the classroom will never make it out into the field.

Demonstrate Your Devotion

You are in a product company, correct? What do product people care about? So show your support by helping sell more products and ensuring that those products are satisfying customers. I'm sure that your services organization is already good at that, but what you may not be good at is continually communicating your contribution to client loyalty, sales growth, and company profitability. Selfishly, this communication is much more important than the actions that spurred it.

You need to constantly show your good citizenship by relentlessly recounting how your services organization helped win key product sales. Quantify your contribution. Record the number and the size of product sales that your services organization helped get. Come up with a formula for showing how your great services work helped retain customers and the amount of business your services organization "saved." Don't whine about how your financial results suffered from bailing out the product screw-ups or giveaways; just point out your contribution in time and dollars for the "good of the corporation." This is where the term "good team player" comes in. Deposit the goodwill of your product brethren into your savings account; there will be times when you will need to make withdrawals, but use this sparingly.

Cater to the Customer
In the early days of your services organization, customers will be skeptical. In some situations, you will be asking them to pay for what was free in the past. In other situations, you may be asking them to buy high-level professional services to be delivered by the same people who provide break-fix services. (What suddenly made them so smart?) Customers will rightly question your capabilities. It is vital that you clearly define your value proposition, market message, and selling approach.

So, above all else, make sure you do a great job with the customer first. If not, the sales force will abandon you. Everyone is watching your organization under the microscope during the first 90 days or so. Your customer relationships will be key to your long-term success, so start now doing what it takes to create some showcase accounts that will support you as your organization matures and gets ready for future success.

> GIST: The step of Survive is all about doing first things first—buying some time while you create the core capabilities required for top performance. Do what is mentioned above, and you'll be around to take advantage of future opportunities.

Step Four: Thrive

With your basic requirements needed to survive as a services leader in a product-driven company in place, it is time to make your services organization thrive, whether your product organization is successful or not! Here are the steps to stepping up:

Open Up Your Offerings

The fate of many services organizations in product companies is almost entirely reliant upon product sales. When product sales are up, the services organization is busy installing or servicing or supporting, resulting in good revenue contribution and solid consultant or customer engineer utilization. However, the flip side is that when product sales slump, services organization performance dips predictably two to three months later; the cough from sales ends up as the "90-day flu" for services. Good excuse or not, you won't make your targets. Your destiny is directly tied to product sales performance. Not reassuring is it?

So take charge of your future by opening up your offerings and creating and selling services that are not directly connected to your product. As outlined in detail in Chapter 5, go talk to your best customers and ask them about their issues, needs, wants, and expectations beyond your products that your services organization has the capabilities to meet. Define these new offerings, test them, then gradually introduce them (using your own people) to other customers who will probably share the same needs (Alexander, 2003). Oftentimes good places to start are assessments, training, certifications, and audits; in essence, all services that easily can be created that build upon existing expertise. Make a goal of having 20% to 35% of your services portfolio offerings non-product-dependent. This will give you both the flexibility and the control to meet your numbers even when the product side is having a tough time.

Protect Your People

The more successful your services organization, the more your organization will be seen as a potential threat to others in the organization. Folks from the product side who have been used to having their way may not appreciate making way for the "services upstarts." Politics are politics, and once people from the services organization are seen as competitors for funds, favors, or fame, they become vulnerable to the passions and ploys of politics.

For example, proficient, dedicated services marketing is an absolute necessity of a successful services organization. When I am involved in assessing services organizations, services marketing is always one of the top three challenges they face. However, what is the expected response when corporate marketing learns that there is a "marketeer" in the company who doesn't report to marketing? Outrage at this blasphemy! No matter how logical and practical it is, you have now created a threat to an often powerful group. Without your vigilant oversight, people assuming this services marketing role are subject to ongoing harassment.

So think about the possible implications of all your actions on other key stakeholders in the organization. Some professional services vice presidents avoid this probable confrontation through creativity by calling their services marketers "business development specialists," or "services quality support," or any other name that doesn't sound like marketing. Yes, it is a little deceptive, but anything that protects your people is good. Others choose to sidestep the issue by outsourcing their services marketing needs, thus keeping control of a critical capability and ignoring battles over headcounts or reporting.

Decipher the Differences

Most product companies have very well-defined and commonly accepted measures of performance. A CFO of a high-tech firm will quickly grasp the financials presented by the CFO of a heavy industries manufacturing organization and vice versa. Although a few of the terms are different, they speak the same Queen's English and use the same Oxford dictionary for definitions.

Yet, the rules of performance tracking for services businesses are different—way different. While "cost of goods" is important to both product and services companies, the inputs of calculation vary tremendously. Whereas return on invested capital (ROIC) or return on capital employed (ROCE) may be highly appropriate for a manufacturer, they are virtually meaningless for a services business where utilization rates and project scope management often are better indicators of performance. However, the folks running the show don't know that, and they probably don't care.

So you need to translate the uniqueness of services business in ways that the product folks will accept (not necessarily understand). The vital person you must have on your side is the CFO. If the top financial person understands the services value you offer, he or she will put it into terms that the CEO will accept. This is a must.

Sell, Sell, Sell

You might have thought your primary responsibilities were to lead, manage, and coach your services team. Yes, these things are all important, but they pale in comparison to your vital success role, which is selling. To make your services organization thrive in a product-centric company, you must sell key customers on your services organization's ability to deliver.

You must sell your team on the vital role they play, and sell them on continuing to excel even when internal circumstances dampen morale. You must sell everyone in the rest of your organization on why your services organization is important, how it contributes to overall success, and why they should change their ways to allow it to make them successful. This is your primary role. Tape three words on the inside of your laptop: Sell, sell, sell. Nothing else will determine your destiny better than this one vital skill.

In addition, you must sell your team on selling services. To truly succeed, you must have (at least a percentage of) the product sales organization on your side. Your consultants in the field are the vital link. Tom Birklund, director of professional services for Diebold, knows this well:

> *My systems engineers use their technical expertise to help sell our customers the services and solutions they need. Yet, even more important, the system engineers are constantly selling the product salespeople on the importance of professional services to the customer and to Diebold. We provide selling skills training for our system engineers and invite product salespeople to attend. This is a great way to get everyone on board the services bandwagon.*

Sounds like a great approach to me.

GIST: The step of Thrive is about putting it all together, harvesting the crop of earlier plantings, and reaping the benefits of previous toil. If you open up your offerings, protect your people, decipher the differences, and sell, sell, sell, you and your services organization will flourish.

Step Five: Evangelize

Now it is time for the fun stuff. Now that you've built up the necessary credibility and have consistently delivered large amounts of profitable revenue, it is time to take things to the next level. As Frank Sinatra used to croon, it's time to "start spread-

ing the news." I will provide some actions you can take to preach the gospel of services throughout your entire organization—how to evangelize the power of being a services-led business.

Find the Figures

Senior management is a data-driven group, so the first step in concocting the case is building the base by finding the figures. To convince senior management, you need quantifiable examples of the trend toward services and the contribution of services to profitable revenue, as well as war stories of product-centric organizations that have made the move from product-centric to services-led. Three approaches help yield this information.

First, start with published studies. If done by reliable sources, they can capsulize key data to make your business case. Look for the reputation of the source, the recency of the data, and the relevance of the information.

Second, do an online search of industry players, top competitors, and other organizations held in high esteem by your top managers. Check their financials over the last three years, looking at services revenue as a percentage of the overall business. Read annual reports to learn their perceptions of issues and the services opportunity. Do a search of recent press releases and speeches to gain insight as to their stance on services. All this can build the services case by demonstrating the trends, opportunities, and possible competitive threats of organizations deemed important by your top brass.

Third, if you think more close-to-home information is needed, do your own market research. Use the voice of the customer to nudge the need and drive the decision to a more services-led business.

Prioritize the Players

The change you are preaching (from product-centric to services-led) is a major transition, one in which some people will perceive that they will win or lose power and/or prestige. There is no way around human nature. Therefore, you must understand this phenomenon in your organization and proactively deal with it. You need to develop traction in the form of a critical mass of influential people who will support your services quest.

Just like any savvy key account executive trying to penetrate an important customer, you need to take a hard look at the key players within your organization. First, identify who they are and think through what you know about their attitudes toward services. Next, plot them on the Influencing Change Continuum illustrated in Figure 31.

Sadly, you probably will have a Resistor or two. Resistors will fight your services initiative, sometimes aggressively. One negative voice from a key stakeholder is often all it takes to kill an initiative, so it is essential to eliminate their resistance. Think about the business issues and personal needs of players in this box, and try to come up with ideas that will move them to the Neutral block. Do whatever you can (within reason) to make the services more acceptable to them. Realistically, you will never get these people to be services Champions or even Supporters, for that matter. Just be happy if you can mute a negative voice.

Although Neutrals won't actively support the move to services, they won't resist it either. Your internal selling strategy here is to nudge them along to become a Supporter. Again, think through what is most important to people who are Neutrals today, and try and make them Supporters tomorrow.

Supporters will do what their classification implies—support

Figure 31

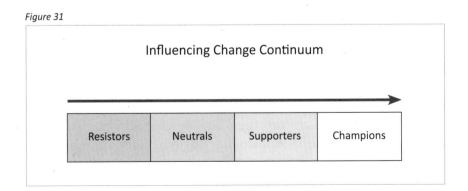

the move to services. They are already on your side and will back your initiative when asked. The strategy here is to get them to be much more proactive, to become a Champion, a flag-waving, pulpit-preaching advocate of the services dream.

Champions are worth their weight in gold. One strong recommendation in a presentation coming from a respected player is worth 20 of your speeches, so nurture and help this select group any way you can.

Build Your Brand

Another very powerful way to evangelize services is to create personal relationships with key customers—those who have the attention of senior management. Actively pursue jointly writing articles about these influential players and presenting case studies about their services success at conferences. Better yet, ask those key customers to jointly write an article with you or co-present at an industry show. This is powerful communication! Make it a point to get to know the movers and shakers in the marketing and industry space you play in. Make your personal brand a part of your industry leadership. Make yourself indispensable.

Market the Message

Start a scrapbook on stories of organizations that "get services right" (the *Professional Services Journal* is a great source), and circulate it to internal players. Take senior managers to attend industry shows, such as Service Strategies' summits and Arizona State University's Center for Services Leadership symposiums, to get better indoctrinated into services. Invite services experts into your organization to share best practices with the true believers (you and your staff) and to separately brief senior management on the global services trends, opportunities, and business implications of transitioning to becoming services-led. Furthermore, these outside services thought leaders can frankly discuss your organization's overall "services readiness" with your organization's leadership to help give them the impetus and the direction for change.

Henrik Moeller-Christensen, former director of services and support for Canon Business Solutions in Europe, knows the importance of marketing the services story internally:

> Historically, we have done a very good job of building our traditional product-support organization. Senior management knows our contribution to both customer satisfaction and profitable revenue. We now are leveraging that past success as we make the business case to get serious about value-added and professional services. I have personally been finding every opportunity to present the services potential to managers within corporate headquarters and within all our country organizations. In addition, I've brought in an outside services expert to tell the services story. Having a highly credible outsider share the benefits of services is a great help in changing the mindset of my senior management colleagues of this mainly product-centric company.

Sage advice for those of us ready to get serious about helping lead the services transition.

The step of Evangelize is all about changing the game from product-centric to services-led. It is the once-in-a-career opportunity to be at the forefront of major organizational change, to lead a transition that can ensure the success of your company. So find the figures, build your brand, prioritize the players, and market your message. This is your chance to truly be a services champion!

Develop an Articulate and Clear Purpose and Rationale

The need for this transition to seriously selling services will not be understood immediately or bought into quickly by many in the organization. As stated earlier, the natural tendency for people is to resist anything new, and some folks (e.g., sales) may be downright antagonistic. People must be sold on the concept over and over again, and a succinct purpose and well-expressed rationale are necessary first steps.

The information you gathered in Step Two to decide/confirm the strategic role of services is helpful in crafting a purpose statement. Here is a straightforward charter for the services business of Chromalox, a 100-year-old product company that decided to tap into the services potential of its industry: "Provide the very best service in the process heat and control industry so that we can have a competitive advantage in selling products...grow as a services business, providing the corporation a reasonable return on investment."

Along with being clear and succinct, this mission statement is non-threatening, as it emphasizes how growing services will be beneficial to growing products.

> GIST: Look for every opportunity to communicate your new services charter with all stakeholders both inside and outside your company.

Inform and Involve All Key Stakeholders

Ponder Point: The best decisions are always your idea.

If there is a secret to successful change, this is it. Everyone who is a stakeholder—those who have something to gain or lose because of the seriously selling services initiative—must have all relevant information presented to them in a way that demonstrates what is being done, why it is being done, and the potential benefits to stakeholders. Furthermore, there is a direct relationship between an individual's involvement with an issue and that person's commitment level to the final outcome. For example, ideally a cross-section of people throughout the organization would have been involved in the strategic assessment described in Step One and the charter creation explained in Step Two.

GIST: Make sure that sales management and a few respected sellers are part of the team involved in the seriously selling services transition.

Change the People Management Systems to Support New Ways of Doing Business

Ponder Point: The fastest way to change performance is to change performance measures.

The new direction means that people are going to have to behave in different (sometimes radically different) ways than they have before. To overcome inertia, all support systems must be changed to expect, encourage, and reward the new behaviors while strongly discouraging operating in business-as-usual mode. The shift to seriously selling services requires different expectations, different objectives, different tools, different processes and procedures, different reward systems...different everything. All elements of people management must be reconsidered before implementation begins.

GIST: What gets expected, inspected, and respected gets done.

Best Practices of Leading Services in a Product Company

1. *Get executive commitment over and over again.* The best time to make your case and to define and negotiate your mission is in the early stages of the game when senior management interest is high and you have some leverage prior to accepting the position. You must take the lead by explaining the three different strate-

gies as defined in Chapter 1, the plusses and minuses of each, and the strategy you propose. It is vital that there are clarity and commitment around the services mission. Driving product sales is fine as long as your task is to grow the service business as well. Service must be a business unit, not a cost center. Furthermore, this is the best time to explain that services must be looked upon as an investment that probably won't make money for the first year (or two, or maybe three), and give the reasons why. This expectation must be understood from the get-go. Also, in order to maintain control of services profitability you must have the CEO telling the sales vice president "you can't do that" every time the sales force wants to give away services for free.

However, even if you've done a great job up front, always be prepared: The economy may change, new executives may be brought in, product sales may start to slump, or key customers may become upset about a new product's performance. Any time there is an organizational change, be prepared to defend the services mission and articulate your value.

2. *Let key customers and hard data make your case.* Talk all you want, but you'll be much more persuasive if you let the voice of key customers and quantitative numbers make the business case for services for you.

3. *Make sure that your first customer engagements go great.* Everyone will be watching you and many will be skeptical. If you don't meet or exceed customer expectations early on, Sales will abandon you. Do whatever it takes to make those initial engagements successful.

4. *Build a strong services leadership team early.* If you are in start-up mode, you have to do everything at once. Yet, you can't do it alone, so identify key positions and gets some very strong, like-minded people in place. For staying power, you have to have strength up the middle.

5. *Take the time to train.* What do you mean you don't have the time or the budget to train your people? Services is a people business, and your people control your fate. Give them the knowledge,

skills, and tools they need to make you successful.

6. *Remember, your primary role is that of a leader of change.* Yes, you need to have strong services management skills, but your main role is to influence, persuade, and sell people inside and outside the organization on the value that your services organization brings. Honing these skills will speed your success.

Conclusion

Through these pages you've learned the many potential benefits of building a services business inside a product company. Results such as new profitable revenue streams, more product sales, and competitive differentiation can be yours as services are built, sold, and delivered the right way. You have learned that there are three services strategies to choose from, and you have been given the knowledge required to select the one most appropriate for your organization.

You've also found out the challenges of turning box pushers into sellers of the invisible and what it takes to overcome them. You've been exposed to the five strategies of how to transition your business from giving services away to getting paid for them, and the plusses and minuses of each. You've discovered the 10 steps to building new, high-value services and what it takes to effectively manage a portfolio of services.

You've been exposed to all the challenges of the channel and the proven approach to getting, finding, and keeping strong services channel partners that will complement your capabilities, allowing you to focus on building distinct, mission-critical competencies.

You've also learned the very unique obstacles in front of being a Stranger in a Strange Land—a services champion tasked with getting the buy-in to services from stakeholders across the board, and then leading services through the five-step maturity model.

Through this book you have been provided tools, approaches, models, and examples of best and worst practices from those who have been there. I've tried to share with you what I've learned over the years through working with some great services people.

Building services inside of product companies is not for the faint of heart. But for those up to the task, it can be a wonderfully fulfilling journey.

Good luck to you all.

References and Notes

Introduction

Alexander, James A. 2004. *The State of Professional Services II: An Industry Comes of Age*. St. James City, FL.: Alexander Consulting.

Chapter 1

Alexander, James A. 2004. *The State of Professional Services II: An Industry Comes of Age*. St. James City, FL.: Alexander Consulting.

Brown, Stephen W., Anders Gustafsson and Lars Witell. 2009. Beyond Products. New York, NY.: *The Wall Street Journal*.

Hahn, Al. 2007. *The True Strategic Value of Services*. Sandy, OR: Hahn Consulting.

Zook, Christopher. 2004. *Beyond the Core: Expand Your Market Without Abandoning Your Roots*. Boston, MA: Harvard Business School Press.

*Note that services margins are declining on average in some industries as more and more services appear alike to customers, are hence seen as commodities, and thus seem to have less value and worth less.

Chapter 3

Alexander, James A. 2007. *Transitioning Technical Experts into Trusted Advisors*. St. James City, FL.: Alexander Consulting.

Chapter 4

*I learned this approach from Steve Lieberson, a top seller for CDI.

Chapter 5

Alexander, James A. 2004. *The State of Professional Services II: An Industry Comes of Age*. St. James City, FL.: Alexander Consulting.

Zeithaml, Valarie A. and Mary Jo Bitner. 2000. *Services Marketing*. New York, NY: McGraw Hill.

Chapter 7

Alexander, James A. 2003. "Amplifying the Voice of the Customer: Launching Profitable Services Right the First Time." *PSO Insights*. St. James City, FL.: Alexander Consulting.

*This was the oft-repeated comment of Detective Joe Friday in the 1950's TV cop show "Dragnet."

Index

About the Author

James A. Alexander, Ed.D, is the founder of Alexander Consulting, a management consultancy that helps product companies create and implement professional services strategies. He researches, publishes, trains, and speaks on the critical issues services leaders face.

Jim has authored or co-authored over 80 articles, three white papers, five research reports, and three books and has taught at universities in the U.S., Europe, and Mexico.

Jim was selected as the services pundit for IBM Global Services 2003 Headlights Program. Furthermore, he served as the U.S. Department of Commerce's e-business subject-matter expert for its Inter-American E-Business Fellowship Program.

Finally, Jim is a trusted advisor and executive coach to many senior executives of leading services organizations, helping them navigate the journey from business-as-usual to business-as-exceptional.

Bring Seriously Selling Services
to Your Organization!

Don't leave your services initiatives to chance, implement the field-proven best practices and benchmarks that are essential for success. Dr. Jim Alexander will share the critical messages contained in his industry best-selling book with your team.

These sessions are available in convenient and flexible for-mats—one-hour speeches, half-day seminars, or full-day workshops—customized for your company.

For more information contact us at:
239-283-7400
alex@alexanderstrategists.com
www.alexanderstrategists.com